Getting in the zone

Here is the cover of a vintage book on the mental aspect of training by "Denie"

Table of contents

Pg 5   Introduction

Pg 15   Chapter 1   The "Super Mental Training book" & "The Training of the Will"

Pg 40   Chapter 2   Some insights from friends

Pg 64   Chapter 3   The wisdom of Dr. Judd

Pg 71   Chapter 4   Some inspiring athlete's stories

Pg 99   Chapter 5   Some Academic wisdom

Pg 120   Chapter 6   Some Old School wisdom

Pg 143   Chapter 7   The Author's take on things

Pg 169   Chapter 8   Ideas from the Martial Arts

Pg 173   Chapter 9   Chimp Strength

Pg 175   Chapter 10   Reaching the sub-conscious

Pg 187   Chapter 11   More Old School stuff

Pg 208   Chapter 12   Sports Psychology

Pg 215   Chapter 13   Summing it all up

Pg 233   Chapter 14   Inspiration Gallery

Great Quote: George S. Patton

Now if you are going to win any battle you have to do one thing. You have to make the mind run the body. Never let the body tell the mind what to do. The body will always give up. It is always tired morning, noon, and night. But the body is never tired if the mind is not tired. When you were younger the mind could make you dance all night, and the body was never tired. You've always got to make the mind take over and keep going.

~George S. Patton, U.S. Army General & 1912 Olympian

I will open with this short bit I wrote quite some time ago which is short and to the point:

Introduction

The Power of Positive Thinking

What is it that has enabled modern day athletes, particularly those in the strength sports, to perform feats that would in years past have been considered impossible? Yes, some of the gains can be attributed to advances in training, equipment & nutrition. I propose that most have come from the power of positive thinking. Cliché yes, but every cliché comes about because of some truth involved. Consider my reasoning here; in the days of Eugene Sandow and his contemporaries, anyone who could bench 300 pounds was considered a phenom. Today, it's no biggie. Has the human body changed that much? No, I don't think so. To the first person that ever benched 300 pounds, it seemed an incredible thing, and at the time, it was. Today, guys are benching 1000 lbs and more, with the modern sophisticated gear available. There seems to be no end in sight. Every time some new record is made, a certain lift is no longer considered the Holy Grail. It's been done, so now it's doable, and the new challenge is to do 10, 20, or 50 pounds more. When this happens, has some sort of physical barrier been removed? No, but a mental one certainly has. Because some individual benched 300, it became possible for others to do it. The mental block was gone. Some positive thinking strongman then posed that he should be able to bench 310. When this was achieved, 320 seemed a reasonable goal. I propose that if we introduced the strongmen of old to the modern world of lifting, that after their initial shock and dismay, within a reasonable time they would smash to bits all of their old personal best lifts. Why??? Because they now believe it to be possible, because it's been done! How many of us have been stuck at or just below a certain round or nice symmetrical number because of a mental block? We were convinced this number held some magical power and it would be very difficult or impossible to overcome. Therefore it was just that. Somehow we kept at it and eventually surprised ourselves by hitting that magic number. Then what happened? For many of us, a steady period of gains ensued until we approached that next big mental barrier we had designed for ourselves. Once again, progress came to a grinding halt. We searched for some new supplement or training technique to help propel us past that new "plateau". When we BELIEVED we had found that certain something, and had a reason to make that new lift, we did it, and lo and behold, a new series of gains came.

To be sure, during this process, the body has gone through some changes. The key thing to keep in mind, however, is that the attitude changed first. The body just followed suit, performing what the mind now demanded and expected of it. We've all heard the stories of the little housewife that lifted the back of a car to free her trapped child. How on earth do we account for that? I think the answer is obvious.

The will has overcome the boundaries of the body.

Of course, positive thinking needs to be backed up by good old fashioned sweat, proper rest, and good nutrition. Set reasonable, short term goals. **Doing 1 more rep here and 5 more pounds there will add up to big things in the long run.** Don't add 100 pounds to your best bench or squat, and think you can positive think it to lockout. But 2 and ½ pounds more or an extra rep is certainly within reason. Don't hold yourself back by creating a barrier that really doesn't exist except in your mind. **Conceive, believe, achieve**!!!!

The following brief article is from this webpage;

http://www.actsweb.org/living/how-grow.php

I found it very interesting & inspirational, and hope that you do as well

Failure: Never Forever

It is well known that for 28 years Abraham Lincoln experienced one failure after another. In 1833 he had a nervous breakdown. When he ran for speaker in 1838 he was defeated. In 1848 he lost re-nomination to Congress and was rejected for land officer in 1849. These failures didn't stop him from battling on. In 1854 he was defeated for the Senate. Two years later he lost the nomination for vice-president and was again defeated for the Senate in 1858. Yet, despite it all, in 1860 he was elected president and went down in history as one of America's greatest presidents. Obviously, success isn't the absence of failure. It is having the determination to never quit because "quitters never win and winners never quit."

Almost every person who has achieved anything worthwhile with his or her life has not only experienced failure but experienced it many times. Lincoln experienced innumerable failures, but he was never a failure because he never gave up. Walt Disney was the same. He went broke several times and had a nervous breakdown before he became successful. Enrico Caruso failed so many times with his high notes that his voice teacher advised him to give up. He didn't. Instead, he persevered and became one of the world's greatest tenors. Albert Einstein and Werner von Braun both failed courses in math. Henry Ford was broke when he was 40. Thomas Edison's school teacher called him a dunce, and later he failed over 6,000 times before he perfected the first electric light bulb.

> "Failure is an event, not a person."

Demosthenes, the famous Greek orator, failed before he became famous. His father died when he was only seven, leaving him a wealthy estate. At age eighteen, through public debate, he sought to claim his estate from his dishonest guardian. Unfortunately, not only was he shy and retiring, but he also had a speech impediment which caused him to fail in trying to prove his right of ownership. Without doubt this failure provided the motivation that gave him the determination to persevere until he became the most famous political orator in antiquity. Nobody knows who received his estate but 2,300 years later students still know about Demosthenes. No matter how badly or how many times a person fails, he is never a failure providing he gets up just one more time than he falls down. Furthermore, like a high jumper, one never discovers his full potential until he reaches his point of failure. As one person said, "Low aim, not failure, is crime." Remember, too that failure is an event, not a person. It is actually the fear of failure, not failure itself that cripples people. As Baudjuin once said, "No matter how hard you work for success, if your thought is saturated with the fear of failure, it will kill your efforts, neutralize your endeavor, and make success impossible." Lincoln, who hated slavery, overcame his many failures to eventually abolish slavery because he had determination, a noble cause to believe in and live for, and the courage to fight for that cause regardless of failures and setbacks. A cause to live for doesn't have to be as mighty as Lincoln's, but does need to be meaningful. Everybody needs something bigger than himself to live for.

> "It is the fear of failure, not failure, which cripples people."

Rather than having no goal, it is, as it has been wisely said, "far better to dare mighty things, to win glorious triumphs, even though checkered with failure, than to take rank with those poor spirits who neither enjoy much nor suffer much, because they live in the gray twilight that knows neither victory nor defeat." It is interesting to know that Lincoln was also a very unhappy and melancholy man. His first sweetheart died before he was able to marry her. And his marriage to Mary Todd would have been enough to destroy any man with less courage and determination than Lincoln. However, historians agree that had Lincoln been happily married, he would never have become president. Out of his failure and unhappiness in marriage he was able to give his life to a great and worthwhile cause. John Wesley, the father of the Methodist church, was another man whose marriage was a failure. He, too, was able to rise above his circumstances to build a work that has helped millions of people around the world. The Apostle Paul was another person with a determination to win. His goal was to proclaim God's message of love and hope to all people. As a result he was thrown into jail several times, and faced death again and again. Five times he was whipped by the Jews and three times he was beaten with rods. Once he was stoned, three times shipwrecked. He faced grave dangers from robbers and mobs. He lived with weariness, pain and sleepless nights. He was often hungry and cold and was criticized for his less-than-perfect looks and speech. But did Paul ever feel that he was a failure or that God had forsaken him? Never! Unwaveringly he kept his eye on his goal.[1] The problems, setbacks and failures along the way strengthened him for the journey. Paul's attitude was: "It is God himself, in his mercy, who has given us this wonderful work [of telling his Good News to others], and so we never give up."[2]

> **"For those who trust in God,
> failure is never forever."**

Now I thought you would like to read some fascinating & little-known history about Abe's young life, which surely built the tenacity required later on...

By Albert Kaplan

Let us read William Herndon's account beginning with a description of Thomas Lincoln, Abraham's father: "He (Thomas Lincoln) was, we are told, five feet ten inches high, weighed one hundred and ninety-five pounds, had a well-rounded face, dark hazel eyes, coarse black hair, and was slightly stoop-shouldered.

His build was so compact that Dennis Hanks used to say that he could not find the points of separation between his ribs ... was sinewy, and gifted with great strength, was inoffensively quiet and peaceable, but when roused to resistance a dangerous antagonist." "It was a wild region, with many bears and other wild animals still in the woods" wrote Lincoln in the Fell autobiography. More details are found in the sketch he furnished John L. Scripps. "He (Thomas Lincoln) settled in an unbroken forest, and this clearing away of the surplus wood was the great task ahead. Abraham, though very young was large of his age, and had an ax (axe) put into his hands at once: and from that till within his twenty-third year he was almost constantly handling that most useful instrument - less, of course, in plowing and harvesting seasons." Herndon reports, "By the time he had reached his seventeenth year he had attained the physical proportions of a full-grown man. He was employed to assist James Taylor in the management of a ferry boat across the Ohio River near the mouth of Anderson's Creek, but was not allowed a man's wages for the work. He received thirty-seven cents a day for what he afterwards told me was the roughest work a young man could be made to do.""In June the entire party, including Offut, boarded a steamboat going up the river. At St. Louis they disembarked, Offut remaining behind while Lincoln, Hanks, and Johnson started across Illinois on foot. At Edwardsville they separated. Hanks going to Springfield, while Lincoln and his step-brother following the road to Coles Country, to which point old Thomas Lincoln had meanwhile removed. Here Abe did not tarry long, probably not over a month, but long enough to dispose most effectively of one Daniel Needman, a famous wrestler who had challenged the returned boatman to a test of strength. The contest took place at a locality known as "Wabash Point". Abe threw his antagonist twice with comparative ease, and thereby demonstrated such marked strength and agility as to render him forever popular with the boys of the neighborhood." "He enjoyed the brief distinction his exhibitions of strength gave him more than the admiration of his friends for his literary or forensic efforts. Some of the feats attributed to him almost surpass belief. One witness declares he was equal to three men, having on a certain occasion carried a load of six hundred pounds. At another time he walked away with a pair of logs which three robust men were skeptical of their ability to carry. "He could strike with a maul a heavier blow - could sink an axe deeper into wood than any man I ever saw." is the testimony of another witness."

(Interrupting Herndon's account for a moment to quote from Browne's biography of Lincoln, on page 53, quoting Dennis Hanks: "My, how he could chop! His ax would flash and bite into a sugar-tree or sycamore, and down it would come. If you heard his fellin' trees in a clearin' you would say there was three men at work by the way the trees fell.") "They (the Clary's Grove boys) conceded leadership to one Jack Armstrong, a hardy, strong, and well-developed specimen of physical manhood, and under him they were in the habit of "cleaning out" New Salem whenever his order went forth to do so. Offut and "Bill" Clary - the latter skeptical of Lincoln's strength and agility - ended a heated discussion in the store one day over the new clerk's ability to meet the tactic of Clary's Grove, by a bet of ten dollars that Jack Armstrong was, in the language of the day, "a better man than Lincoln". The new clerk strongly opposed this sort of an introduction, but after much entreaty of Offut, at last consented to make his bow to the social lions of the town in this unusual way. He was now six feet four inches high, and weighed, as a friend and confident, William Green, tells with impressive precision, "two hundred and fourteen pounds". The contest was to be a friendly one and fairly conducted. All New Salem adjourned to the scene of the wrestle. Money, whisky, knives, and all manner of property were staked on the result. It is unnecessary to go into the details of the encounter. Everyone knows how it ended: how at last the tall and angular rail-splitter, enraged at the suspicion of foul tactics, and profiting by his height and length of his arms, fairly lifted the great bully by the throat and shook him like a rag ...." "Mr. Lincoln's remarkable strength resulted not so much from muscular power as from the toughness of his sinews. He could not only lift from the ground enormous weight, but could throw a cannonball or a maul farther than anyone in New Salem." "No little of Lincoln's influence with the men of New Salem can be attributed to his extraordinary feats of strength. By an arrangement of ropes and straps, harnessed about his hips, he was enabled one day at the mill to astonish a crowd of village celebrities by lifting a box of stones weighing near a thousand pounds." (Interrupting Herndon's account again, on page 154 of Ward H. Lamon's "The Life of Lincoln", one reads "Lincoln has often been seen in the old mill on the river bank to lift a box of stones weighing from one thousand to twelve hundred pounds." In 1998 the University of Illinois Press published "Herndon's Informants", edited by Douglas L. Wilson and Rodney O. Davis. On page 7 is a May 28, 1865 letter to William H. Herndon from his cousin, J. Rowan Herndon.

An excerpt, as written, follows: "... he was By far the stoutest man that I ever took hold of I was a mere Child in his hands and I considered myself as good a man as there was in the Country until he Come about I saw him lift Between 1000 and 1300 lbs of Rock weighed in a Box ..."Continuing Herndon's account: "There is no fiction either, as suggested by some of his biographers, in the story that he lifted a barrel of whisky from the ground and drank from the bung; but in performing this later almost incredible feat he did not stand erect and elevate the barrel, but squatted down and lifted it to his knees ..." "When he walked he moved cautiously but firmly; his long arms and giant hands swung down by his side. He walked with even tread, the inner sides of his feet being parallel. He put his whole foot flat down on the ground at once, not landing on the heal; he likewise lifted his foot all at once, not rising from the toe, and hence he had no spring to his walk. His walk was undulatory - catching and pocketing tire, weariness, and pain, all up and down his person, and thus preventing them from locating. The first impression of a stranger, or a man who did not observe closely, was that his walk implied shrewdness and cunning - that he was a tricky man; but in reality it was the walk of caution and firmness." "From Lincoln's campaign biography we read the following: "In the autumn of 1816 when Abraham was eight years old, his father determined to quit Kentucky. Already the evil influences of slavery were beginning to be felt by the poor and the non-slave-holders. But the emigration of Thomas Lincoln is, we believe, to be chiefly attributed to the insecurity of the right by which he held his Kentucky land; for, in those days, land titles were rather more uncertain than other human affairs. Abandoning his old home, and striking through the forests in a northwesterly direction, he fixed his new dwelling-place in the heart of the "forest primeval" of what is now Spencer County, Indiana. The dumb solitude there had never echoed to the ax, and the whole land was a wilderness." "The rude cabin of the settler was hastily erected, and then those struggles and hardships commenced which are the common trials of frontier life, and of which the story has been so often repeated. Abraham was a hardy boy, large for his years, and with his ax did manful service in clearing the land. Indeed, with that implement, he literally hewed out his path to manhood; for until he was twenty-three, the ax was seldom out of his hand, except in the intervals of labor, or when it was exchanged for the plow, the hoe, or the sickle."

"Returning to Herndon: "Mr. George Close, the partner of Lincoln in the rail-splitting business, says that Lincoln was, at this time, a farm laborer, working from day to day, for different people, chopping wood, mauling rails, or doing whatever was to be done. The country was poor, and hard work was the common lot; the heaviest share falling to the young unmarried men, with whom it was a continual struggle to earn a livelihood. Lincoln and Mr. Close made about one thousand rails together, for James Hawks and William Miller, receiving their pay in homespun clothing. Lincoln's bargain with Miller's wife, was, that he should have one yard of brown jeans, (richly dyed with walnut bark) for every four hundred rails made, until he should have enough for a pair of trousers. As Lincoln was already of great altitude, the number of rails that went to the acquirement of his pantaloons was necessarily immense." The primeval forest of America is no more, nor the men and boys who cleared it. Abraham Lincoln's father, Thomas, was a man of extraordinary strength. "... he could not find the point of separation between his ribs ..." describes a muscularity virtually unknown in the world today. And, Abraham's strength was molded, no less than his father's, by the hardest, sustained physical labor known. Mr. Offut boasted that there was no stronger man in the State of Illinois than his clerk, Abraham Lincoln. And, we read in Richard N. Current's "The Lincoln Nobody Knows" the following: "The strongest man I ever looked at" recalled an Illinoisan who had helped Lincoln with his bath when he was in Galesburg to debate with Stephen A. Douglas (1848)." My favorite description is that of Elliot Herndon, William H. Herndon's brother. He succinctly summed up young Lincoln: "I would say he was a cross between Venus and Hercules". Continuing to quote Richard N. Currrent, we read, "A couple of years before starting the beard he had referred in public, in his self-deprecating way, to his 'poor lean, lank face.'" His nose was prominent and slightly askew, with the tip glowing red, as Herndon noticed. His heavy eyebrows overhung deep eye-caverns in which his eyes - sometimes dreamy, sometimes penetrating - were set. His cheekbones were high, his cheeks rather sunken, his mouth wide, his lips thick, especially the lower one, and his chin upturned. On the right cheek, near his mouth, a solitary mole stood out. His skin was sallow, leathery, wrinkled, dry, giving him a weather-beaten look. He had projecting - some said flapping - ears. His hair was thick and unruly, stray locks falling across his forehead.""

"The foregoing list of traits hardly adds up to a flattering sum. The physical Lincoln, the external man, was made for caricature, was the delight of cartoonists. But there was more, far more, to Lincoln's appearance than all this. He cannot fairly be depicted by a mere catalogue of his peculiarities. To the people he met he made an impression which no such inventory can convey." "At first glance, some thought him grotesque, even ugly, and almost all considered him homely. When preoccupied or in repose he certainly was far from handsome. At times he looked unutterably sad, as if every sorrow were his own, or he looked merely dull, with a vacant gaze. Still, as even the caustic Englishman Dicey observed, there was for all his grotesqueness, "an air of strength, physical as well as moral, and a strange look of dignity" about him. And when he spoke a miracle occurred. "The dull, listless features dropped like a mask." according to Horace White, an editor of the *Chicago Tribune*. "The eyes began to sparkle, the mouth to smile, the whole countenance was wreathed in animation, so that a stranger would have to said, "Why this face, so angular and somber a moment ago, is really handsome!" "He was the homeliest man I ever saw." said Donn Piatt, and yet there was something about the face that Piatt never forgot. "It brightened, like a lit lantern, when animated." "Here was a Lincoln the camera never caught. When he went to the studio and sat before the lens he invariably relapsed into his sad, dull, abstracted mood. No wonder, he had to sit absolutely still, with his head against the photographer's rack, while the tedious seconds ticked by. It took time to get the image with the slow, wet-plate process of those days. There was no candid camera, no possibility of taking snapshots which might have recorded Lincoln at his sparkling best. "I have never seen a picture of him that does anything like justice to the original." said Henry Villard, the *New York Herald* reporter. "He is a much better looking man than any of the pictures represent." "The portrait painters were hardly more successful. "Lincoln's features were the despair of every artist who undertook his portrait." his private secretary John G. Nicolay declared. A painter might measure the subject, scrutinize him in sitting after sitting, and eventually produce a likeness of a sort. But "this was not he who smiled, spoke, laughed, charmed." said Nicolay. The poet Walt Whitman commented after getting a close-up view: "None of the artists or pictures have caught the subtle and indirect expression of this man's face." And again, some years after Lincoln's death: "Though hundreds of portraits have been made, by painters and photographers (many to pass on, by copies, to future times),

I have never seen one yet that in my opinion deserved to be called a perfectly good likeness: nor do I believe there is really such a one in existence." "The word pictures do much to supply what the photographs and paintings missed, yet these descriptions also fail to show the man complete. All who tried to describe him admitted that the phenomenal mobility and expressiveness of his features, the reflections of his complex and wide-ranging personality, were beyond the power of words. "The tones, the gestures, the kindling eye, and mirth-provoking look defy the reporter's skill." the reporter Noah Brooks confessed after seeing Lincoln deliver the Cooper Union speech (1860)." "Beyond a certain point Lincoln's appearance not only defied description; it also baffled interpretation. "There is something in the face which I cannot understand." said Congressman Henry L. Dawes of Massachusetts. And the leader of the German-Americans in Illinois, Gustave Koerner, remarked: "Something about the man, the face is unfathomable. In his looks there were hints of mysteries within." Here is a rare description of Lincoln in the early 1840's, taken from the October 3, 1955 issue of "Lincoln Lore": "The summer edition of the Journal of the Illinois State Historical Society has contributed an extremely valuable world portrait of Abraham Lincoln preliminary to his congressional term. Harmon Y. Reynolds edited the "Masonic Towell" published in Springfield, Illinois and shortly after the assassination of the President prepared an editorial for the issue of May 15, 1865, which opened with the statement that he had known Lincoln "ever since 1840". The paragraph in which he described Lincoln in the early forties follows:" "The people are accustomed to look upon Mr. Lincoln as he appeared when elected President. The pictures and photographs that meet the eye everywhere, even when flattering him, by no means do justice to his appearance in early manhood. The first time we saw him to know him, he rose to address the House. His figure was tall, and his face sufficiently full to relieve the prominences so noticeable in later life. Although dark, yet his face was fresh, almost to floridness, his eye was brilliant and speaking (sparkling), his hair was heavy and well-dressed, and greatly added to his appearance. No man in the house seemed to care so little for dress, and yet no one dressed in better taste. Humor, mercy, and talent were ineffaceably delineated upon his countenance." Lincoln described how, in the early 1840's, he appeared to voters who knew him only by his appearance.

In a letter to Martin M. Morris, dated March 26, 1843, he wrote, "It would astonish if not amuse, the older citizens to learn that I (a stranger, friendless, uneducated, penniless boy, working on a flatboat at ten dollars per month) have been put down here as the candidate of pride, wealth, and aristocratic family distinction." I will now close this review by briefly mentioning the daguerreotype image of the young man. Forensic science confirms its bonefides. The young man is Lincoln. In fact, there is no possibility he is not Lincoln. Because as a child Lincoln suffered a traumatic blow to the head with consequential facial deformities, we are offered unique points of identification which, if present in the Kaplan daguerreotype, would be ponderous evidence. And, it is all there, clearly, plainly. These unique, trauma-induced peculiarities of Lincoln's face (masterfully analyzed by Dr. Edward J. Kempf., "Abraham Lincoln's Organic and Emotional Neurosis", American Medical Association Archives of Neurology and Psychiatry, April 1952, Volume 67, Number 4, pp. 419-433; and "Abraham Lincoln's Philosophy of Common Sense", New York Academy of Sciences, 1965, Volume I, Chapter I, pp. 1-18.) are seen, unmistakably, in the daguerreotype.

The following excerpt is from an older book called "The Super Mental Training Book"

The Author Robert K. Stevenson, N.D., researched The Super Mental Training Book for over 15 years. Formerly an elite level athlete himself, Dr. Stevenson talked to hundreds of sports champions and others to discover what mental training strategies worked and why. His findings, contained in this book, tell you all you need to know and do to become a consistent winner and achieve your full athletic potential.

THE SUPER MENTAL TRAINING BOOK

The Super Mental Training Book came about because Bob Stevenson possesses a unique background. He is, first of all, a competitive athlete in several sports. He has participated in the National Outdoor Racquetball Championships, California Handball Championships, dozens of tennis tournaments in the "Open" and "B" divisions, as well as many long-distance races and track meets. Dr. Stevenson played varsity tennis at California State University, Fullerton, and is the author of several books, including "The Golden Era of Preventive Medicine" and "Backwards Running." Of his four college degrees, his doctorate is in Naturopathy (the science of healing without drugs or surgery), and his Master's is in Social Science. He has had, in short, constant exposure to the athletic world, and this, combined with his expertise in health and psychology, has formed the foundation for The Super Mental Training Book. Applying his in-depth knowledge of mental rehearsal techniques, Dr. Stevenson taught self-hypnosis to more than 20 athletes during the mid-1970s. Most of them produced outstanding athletic performances while using self-hypnosis; some setting national records in the process. This positive outcome fueled the author's desire to write a mental training book to which professional and weekend athletes alike could turn for guidance and motivation. Dr. Stevenson reasoned that such a book needed to be more than an academic treatment of one mental rehearsal technique after another (what typically is encountered in other sports psychology type books). He believed that the reader would be most influenced by testimonials of known athletes. Certainly the words and stories of Jack Nicklaus, Wade Boggs, Martina Navratilova, and other sports champions, citing their successful experiences with mental training, would prove more useful and inspirational than any presentation of theoretical concepts. Furthermore, by bringing the experience of such stars into a personal frame of reference, it would let even the most casual athlete realize the potential of such techniques.

This approach added years to Dr. Stevenson's project. The result is, however, what I believe to be a magnificent product of genius and perseverance. I strongly recommend The Super Mental Training Book to anyone interested in active sports. You wish to improve, I'm sure. In this book you will learn how the application of various mental training strategies has brought championships, records, and greatness to many athletes. More important, though, is to learn how you yourself can profit from these easy-to-use methods. Once this realization is clear, act upon it. For your athletic performances, and life, will then attain a new level of accomplishment and satisfaction.

(INTRODUCTION)

Attending Mental Training Workshops

(Few athletes and coaches do this thereby allowing astute opponents who do participate in these to gain a mental edge come the competition; see Kurt Krueger's experience) Being Your Own Mental Coach (Dr. Kroger says that auto- suggestions are much more meaningful to a person than suggestions "given to him by someone else," such as a coach/sports psychologist) Autosuggestions (Should be done every day, and on the day they compete, the suggestions being fresh and tailor-made; periodic reinforcement beneficial, says Dr. Kroger)

Mental Training Sessions

(Naruse taught 125 Japanese Olympians self-hypnosis, resulting in increased confidence and improved performances; the author promotes regular practice of self-hypnosis, visualization, or other mental disciplines of interest, estimating that 95% of all athletes do not engage in mental training;

Dr. Kroger advocates 6 short self-hypnosis sessions per day; lactic acid level usually falls during mental training) Avoidance of Drugs, Marijuana (Hypnotist Pat Collins requires her students to stay off pot, having found that drug users rarely master self- hypnosis, because they do not practice; Dr. Reedy notes that Oakland Raiders who were "regular users were usually gone by the end of the year," their motivation having disintegrated; Cleveland Browns coach Sam Rutigliano saw drug-using players lose their discipline)

Applying the Instant Self-hypnosis Capability (If necessary, one can give himself reinforcing autosuggestions during time outs and breaks in the action. Golf legend Jack Nicklaus says, "Form a positive picture in your mind of how the ball must behave to drop into the hole, then stick to your plan as you set up to and stroke the ball." Meanwhile, another great golf champion, Tom Watson, declares that "the most important aspect of any shot is to visualize what you want to do before you address the ball and swing."

Ken Norton, former world heavyweight boxing champion, once observed, "By the time I get to the fight everything is embedded in my subconscious. Then, if an opportunity presents itself during the fight, it's an automatic reflex." Tennis's Martina Navratilova informs us, "Especially if I've got a grudge match, or I want to prove something, win something big, I will go to sleep imagining what I am going to do. I try to envision the kind of points I want to be playing, the feeling of euphoria after the win, everything." Men's tennis champion, Ivan Lendl, by contrast, remarks that "I practice to music because it gives you rhythm and inspires you to play your best. I have speakers in the trees and on my practice court and I seem to play my best matches when one of my favorite songs sticks in my mind." One of baseball's premier hitters, George Brett, recalls what he did while recovering from an injury during the 1980 season: "I'd sit on the bench and visualize myself at the plate. I must have batted 600 times in my mind." What are all these sports superstars talking about? They are, of course, referring to mental training strategies; strategies which have helped each achieve his or her full athletic potential. Over the years many top athletes have used self-hypnosis, visualization, meditation, music, and other mental rehearsal techniques to dramatically improve their athletic performance. The resulting outstanding performances have often led to world records and championships. You read about the world records and money won by these athletes, but little is said about their mental training regimens. Yet, as far as most athletes are concerned, this is the story which should be reported. For the mass of evidence clearly indicates that self-hypnosis, visualization, and other mental disciplines can help the average athlete, top athlete, any athlete achieve his potential; and realizing one's full potential is the logical, ultimate goal. In this book I am going to tell you about the mental training strategies used by scores of sports champions, including the Soviet Olympic athletes, and their successes (and occasional failures) while employing these techniques. I am going to report this behind-the-scenes story in greater detail than ever before attempted, noting at times the mistakes and blunders some have made in seeking mental training's benefits. You will see that there are simple mental procedures you can easily learn and practice which will substantially improve your game, as well as help you in everyday life. Especially if you are a junior athlete, you can use these procedures to transform your emotional outbursts into precision victories; you will play with confidence and total concentration, and make things rough for your opponent. For coaches, the bottom line is that the mental techniques discussed here, when properly implemented, will enable your players to win more often. You will learn that the "best" mental discipline is the one you feel most comfortable in practicing, and which generates the greatest positive results for you. Some athletes swear by self-hypnosis, some like visualization, others favor meditation, and so on. Every person is different, and possesses his own preferences and inclinations. So, choose from the dozens of mental procedures presented in this book one or more you feel might help you, and see what happens.

Before you embark on this course of action, though, you might wish to profit from a clearer understanding of the role mental training now plays in sports. The balance of this chapter offers a useful context with which to view mental training, describes some of its features, and highlights an effective and powerful mental rehearsal technique. Pioneering Work on the Use of Hypnosis by Athletes in 1972, a book was published which has virtually gone unnoticed: **The Use of Hypnosis in Athletics, by Dr. Wilfred M. Mitchell**. The book is one of those pioneering efforts which contain virtues and deficiencies in equal measure. I shall not review all the book's contents, but will give you some idea of what it is about. Dr. Mitchell lists three purposes of his book: (1) "to bring into the open forum of public discussion" the topic of the use of hypnosis in athletics; (2) to report the findings of a survey Dr. Mitchell sent to high schools, junior colleges, colleges, and universities in the U.S. and Canada. The survey, conducted in 1969, mainly tried to determine how much and how often athletes in these schools used hypnosis; and (3) "to contribute an opening statement in the discussion of the use of hypnosis in athletics by approving its use when done intelligently" These purposes are laudable, but Dr. Mitchell's book hardly created a ripple. One major reason for this was that the book could be obtained only by ordering it from the Department of Psychology, University of the Pacific, an obscure marketing concern to say the least. It is not surprising, therefore, that hardly anyone knows the book exists. Dr. Mitchell obtained his information from a questionnaire. He sent the form to 1641 colleges and universities across the country. A disappointing total of 422 schools replied. Of these only 76 reported instances where some of their athletes had used hypnosis. Furthermore, it is not known who filled out the questionnaire. The Athletic Director's secretary, a part-time coach, the athlete himself, we simply do not know. Obviously, it is important that affected athletes directly participate in any such questionnaire project. It seems that the only meaningful way to reasonably estimate how many athletes use hypnosis, visualization, and similar mental rehearsal techniques, and how often they practice these tech- niques, is to talk to the athlete himself! No matter how perfectly designed, a questionnaire sent to an athletic department probably does not get any farther than the Athletic Director's secretary. Tracking down the athlete and talking to him does require a lot of effort, but it is by far the most rewarding way to research the subject. For the last 15 years, I have talked to hundreds of athletes. The overwhelming majority of them have never used self-hypnosis, visualization, or other mental preparation procedures. However, I discovered quite a few who do. These athletes, forming the minority, besides telling me of their experiences with mental training, related several incredible stories that come out only through personal contact. Dr. Mitchell's study uncovered 76 instances of athletes using hypnosis, but the names of these athletes who employed the technique were not given. If we do not know their names, we cannot confirm the facts. It is advisable therefore that we find athletes who are willing to publicly discuss their use of mental training strategies; and, I have found that if we approach in person athletes reported or rumored to use mental disciplines, most likely they will openly discuss their experiences. This direct approach proved truly helpful because whenever I had questions about certain details of a testimonial later on, I could go back to the athlete and doublecheck the actual situation. I should mention that a few professional athletes would not speak to me about their mental training experiences; even though the information was already public knowledge (had been reported in newspapers and magazines). But, these closed mouths constituted less than a handful. Every other athlete I approached was willing and eager to tell his story. Bruce Ogilvie, a sports psychologist at San Jose State University, who has worked as a consultant for the Dallas Cow- boys, Philadelphia '76ers, and several other professional sports teams, says that "athletes don't want people to know they've had shrinks in their lives. It's very dangerous to do that. There's the implication that you didn't do it all yourself and it could imply that you had some severe emotional problems. Again, contrary to what Dr. Ogilvie indicates, most of the athletes interviewed were not reluctant to discuss their mental training regimens and sessions with "shrinks."

Number of Athletes "Into" Self-hypnosis, Visualization, and Other Mental Disciplines

How many athletes use self-hypnosis, visualization, meditation, or other mental training strategies? An actual number is really not possible to obtain. Based on my research, however, I estimate that no more than 5% of professional and amateur athletes regularly use any of these effective techniques. Even if 5% is an incorrect figure, it is not off by more than a factor of two and simply indicates that too few athletes engage in mental training to improve their athletic performance. As for the other 95%, they generally rely on haphazard traditional methods, such as the locker room pep talk, to prepare for competition. In fact, many athletes in this group do not even bother to "psych up." This is understandable given: (1) the unreliability and ineffectiveness of haphazard methods, and (2) the superficial level of consciousness which these traditional methods address. At the elite athlete level mental training is becoming much more commonplace nowadays, but it still has not permeated to any great extent to the lower athletic ability levels. In certain quarters interest in mental training remains at historic lows. For instance, Dr. Kurt Krueger, a sports psychologist, conducted a Practical Sports Psychology Workshop at Orange Coast College in April, 1985. Dr. Krueger presented at his workshop ways for one to practice and teach such mental disciplines as visualization and meditation. The point behind learning such disciplines, according to the sports psychologist, is that "if you have techniques that you can consciously practice to get into a peak experience, then you can have a peak (athletic) performance more at will." [2] No doubt Dr. Krueger 's workshop had a lot to offer, and it only cost $25 to attend. Nonetheless just 10 people showed up for it. This is the type of situation one still encounters in searching for evidence of widespread or growing interest in mental training.

Naruse's Scientific Study

Many scientific papers have been published about athletes employing self-hypnosis, or other mental disciplines, and experiencing an improvement in their performance. An example of these is Gosaku Naruse's study, "The Hypnotic Treatment of Stage Fright in Champion Athletes" (see International Journal of Clinical and Experimental Hypnosis, April, 1965, Vol. VIII, Number 2, pp. 63-70). Naruse worked with 125 Japanese athletic champions who had returned to the country from the Rome Olympics in 1960." His mission was "to utilize hypnosis for the therapeutic treatment of stage fright" in these athletes. He had been requested to do this by the Training Committee of the Japanese Society for Physical Culture. Naruse taught the athletes "self- training, a form of hypnosis" which he claims "had an excellent therapeutic effect on stage fright and the athlete's confidence." Later on in his paper, Naruse goes through individual case histories, a typical one being this: Case G. Free pistol champion, 35 years old, male. He showed a great interest in the group learning autogenic training; but because of his intense concentration he had to be helped with heterohypnosis in order to experience heaviness and warmth. (In one competition) he was too emotionally disturbed to achieve the sensation of heaviness and warmth. (He then) asked his trainer to come and stand behind him at the shooting position. He recovered his ability for self-control and relaxation and became calm. He performed wonderfully in the match. Afterwards he told the trainer that at that critical moment he felt as if he were hypnotized by the trainer, who suggested calmness and encouraged him to have self-confidence. Naruse never reveals the identity of this free pistol champion, nor reveals the identities of all the other athletes to whom he taught his version of self-hypnosis. Of course, this is protocol in a scientific paper; but, while this might make for good science etiquette, it does not inspire the average athlete who chances upon Naruse' s paper to try out hypnosis. "Free pistol champion" is simply too vague. So, if we are ever going to deliver an effective message to athletes about the benefits of self-hypnosis, visualization, and the like, we must be as specific as possible. In this book I will be as specific as possible.

Appropriateness of Self-hypnosis, Visualization, and Meditation

Before I describe some of the characteristics of the various mental disciplines athletes use, let me address certain questions I have been asked. First of all, it is legal in every state in the U.S. for you to learn and practice self-hypnosis, visualization, meditation, and similar mental rehearsal techniques on your own. Generally speaking, you will also be violating no laws if, for instance, you hypnotize a fellow athlete for the purpose of helping him play better. There is one state, Kansas, which has an outdated statute on the books that possibly forbids this. According to Robert A. Romanoff, the Kansas law states that "to allow oneself to be hypnotized can result in up to thirty days in jail and/or a fine not exceeding $500."

But, this type of law is highly unusual. It is only when you start charging money for hypnotizing others, or use hypnosis and related mental disciplines in a way that might be construed as the practice of medicine, that you must be aware of various restrictions (local ordinances, the Business and Professions Code, and so on). However, avocational uses of mental training techniques, about which we are concerned in this book, attract little attention by any authority. "Avocational use of mental training techniques" means practicing them as a hobby, or only occasionally, for purposes of self-improvement or relaxation. It is appropriate, therefore, to hypnotize a friend, for example, assuming you do it for free, and it is for the purpose of helping your friend with his sports, studies, or something else worthwhile. Along these lines, I advise athletes to develop a self-hypnosis, self-visualization, or self-meditation capability. One reason is because, having attained this type of capability, it costs you nothing to employ. By contrast, a half hour session with a sports psychologist or hypnotist currently averages $50 and that is getting off cheap. Some of the top sports psychologists with whom I have talked charge $125 or more a session! Sports superstars can afford such an outlay; but, it is not necessary for you to spend such sums. You can learn and practice self-hypnosis, visualization, or meditation on your own with no difficulty. Usually all that is required to get started is for you to read a book or article which describes these techniques and their mastery, and then give it a go; this, in fact, is how many champion athletes learned their preferred mental disciplines. Hopefully, this book will serve you in the same capacity.

You Are Your Own Best Coach

Another reason why you should learn and regularly apply some mental discipline is because you are your own best coach. You know better than anyone else what mental, physical, and technical aspects of your game or event need work. You are, therefore, more likely to carry out your own advice than someone else's. After all, it is a rare coach who knows you and your needs that well (let alone cares about you and your needs that much). Dr. William J. Kroger, author of the most comprehensive textbook on hypnosis, Clinical and Experimental Hypnosis (1977), agrees that the individual is more willing to respond to his own suggestions. Dr. Kroger states, "When a person suggests thoughts to himself, this is much more meaningful than when they are given to him by someone else." It is also unlikely your coach will know anything about mental training strategies, such as the use of hypnosis or visualization. So, to properly prepare yourself mentally, it is best to develop and draw on your own resources. Now, self-hypnosis, visualization, and meditation do not guarantee you victory or even a good performance. Most of the time they will provide you an outstanding frame of mind for competition. There will be a few occasions, however, where these techniques will seemingly not help you at all. When this happens, often it is not the fault of the techniques, but rather some underlying cause. You may be fed up with competition, burned out or stale, for example.

Self- hypnosis, visualization, and meditation are not going to do a good job of psyching you up if that is the way you really feel. Also, if you are out of shapes, playing with a cold or otherwise ill, do not expect mental rehearsal techniques to come to the rescue. You will be able to expend a certain amount of energy, and then that is it. As Dr. Kroger observes, "There is no danger that an athlete will go beyond his physiologic limit. The built-in or involuntary reflexes protect the individual against danger at all levels." To perform at your best you need to be in top mental condition and in top physical condition! Serious athletes generally have no trouble getting in excellent physical condition; it is the mental part which gives them the most headaches. While we are primarily concerned in this book with the mental conditioning necessary for peak athletic performance, let us not minimize the importance of physical conditioning. You simply have to be in shape if you want to do well in your sport.

Forget Mental Training If You Are a Marijuana or Drug User

Self-hypnosis, visualization, and meditation are not going to prove of much help if you are a user of marijuana or drugs. Pat Collins, Hollywood's "hip" hypnotist, requires all her students enrolled in her self-hypnosis classes to stay off pot and drugs. This is because the individual's motivation is sapped by the effects of marijuana- smoking or drug-taking. According to Collins, four out of five of her students enjoy success with self-hypnosis. "The other 20% who fail to get results," she notes, "do not practice." Drug users and marijuana smokers, unfortunately, develop a lack of self-discipline to continue practicing self-hypnosis or other mental training techniques; a phenomenon many, including myself, have witnessed. There is convincing scientific data to explain the inability to concentrate and motivate oneself when on pot. Dr. Hardin Jones, in his book Sensual Drugs, relates in detail how a person's brain functions are seriously, and often permanently, damaged by marijuana ;harm which occurs even if one smokes pot but once of twice a week. Explains Dr. Jones in part: The (marijuana) user's psychomotor coordination is impaired. He may suffer illusions and hallucinations, difficulty in recalling events in the immediate past, slowed thinking and narrowed attention span, depersonalization, euphoria or de- pression, drowsiness or insomnia, difficulty in making accurate self-evaluation, a lowering of inhibition, a loss of judgment, and mental and physical lethargy. It should be apparent that an athlete, lethargic and "not all there" from smoking marijuana or indulging in even more destructive drugs such as cocaine, will neglect practicing self-hypnosis or other mental disciplines; he will also likely neglect his physical conditioning and assignments associated with his sport, fading away into a mediocre athlete, former athlete, or worse. This is exactly what Sam Rutigliano, former Cleveland Browns head coach, discovered. He noted: In my experience with players on drugs, the first thing they lose is their discipline during meetings. A player on drugs is not going to be able to respond to the tests he has to take. He's not going to be able to practice well. He's not going to be able to play well.

He's going to be a little late for this and a little late for that. As Coach Rutigliano's observation illustrates, coaches who kick drug users off the team are totally justified in their action, and need make no apologies. The justifications are many, one of them being that the user might recruit other team members into the drug scene; such entrapment happens all the time nowadays, usually behind the coaches' and families' backs, and is one of the saddest developments in sports. One reason I have dwelled on the drugs and marijuana issue is to highlight the importance motivation plays in the practicing of and benefitting from self-hypnosis, visualization, and meditation. Drugs and marijuana, by diminishing the athlete's motivation and overall energy level, just do not mix with mental training. As Dr. Kroger points out, the effectiveness of self-hypnosis "depends upon strong motivation, the intelligent application of the autosuggestions, and diligence: these are the essential prerequisites."

Similarities between Self-hypnosis and Meditation

I have referred to self-hypnosis and meditation in the same breath so far because basically they are the same thing. Self-hypnosis and meditation produce similar physiologic effects on the body. This was confirmed by Larry C. Walrath and David W. Hamilton, whose experiments showed that "autohypnosis and meditation produce similar effects on autonomic arousal. Some of these similar effects included a lower heart rate and lower breathing rate.

Interestingly, a control group who did not use self-hypnosis or meditation but instead was just told to relax, also experienced a lower heart and breathing rate. This led the experimenters to state that "the effects of meditation can be replicated by simple instruction." [12] Self-hypnosis and meditation, if they can be said to differ at all, do so mainly in the frame of mind they provide. In meditation you ordinarily clear your mind of all thoughts, and emerge from the session experiencing a general sense of well-being. You can do the same thing with self-hypnosis, but self-hypnosis practitioners usually strive for more than just relaxation. Athletes who use self-hypnosis often give themselves hypnotic suggestions which intensify their competitiveness and aggressiveness, for example, "Today, I will play as hard as I can. I will totally dominate my opponent and win!" These types of suggestions are somewhat strong, but by and large they are effective; athletes into self-hypnosis do not hesitate implanting their subconscious with such thoughts. Along these lines, Dr. Warren R. Johnson notes that "athletes seem happy with the idea of suggestions which would encourage them to be more aggressive in a sportsmanlike way. This is not surprising, for serious athletes thrive on putting out; they are not in sports to surrender to their opponent, or walk away knowing they could have done better. Just as self-hypnosis and meditation are pretty much the same thing, so too are other mental techniques favored by certain athletes 'techniques such as visualization, imagery, biofeedback, and yoga.

Visualization, a mental discipline currently popular with Olympic athletes and sports psychologists, calls for you to: (1) picture in your mind the way you want to perform an action, and/or feel yourself performing the desired action. For best results, you generally practice visualization while in a relaxed state and with your eyes closed (the same holds true for self-hypnosis and meditation). Imagery is the same thing as visualization; it is a term sports psychologists operating at the college level seem to prefer. We shall investigate visualization, biofeedback, and yoga in greater detail in later chapters. For now it is sufficient to note that there is one highly important physiologic benefit any mental rehearsal technique can provide the athlete: the lowering of the lactic acid level in the muscles and blood. Lactic acid, the "fatigue acid," is the waste product created by the muscles during exertion. If you exercise hard enough and long enough, lactic acid accumulates in your tissues and blood to such an extent that you finally experience fatigue. The high lactic acid level in your body inhibits or prevents your muscles from contracting. A lactic acid level concentration in your muscle fibers of about 0.3% makes further physical activity virtually impossible. However, you can significantly reduce the accumulation of lactic acid in your body during competition. Herbert Benson points out in his informative book, The Relaxation Response (1975), Introduction that "blood-lactate levels fall rapidly during the first ten minutes of meditation." Ordinarily, after hard exercise the lactic acid level in your body takes an hour or longer to return to normal. This is too long a time period, though, to help you during a game. But, keep in mind that you can meditate during halftime, time outs, or breaks. In this fashion you can dramatically lower the lactic acid level in your body, which is a good employment of time while you are waiting for competition to resume. Quite a few sports champions, in fact, follow this strategy.

Self-hypnosis for the Athlete

Because all mental rehearsal techniques contain elements of hypnosis, let us take a closer look at self-hypnosis (autosuggestion), how one can learn it, and how the athlete can benefit from it. To begin with, we should define hypnosis. Naturally, there are as many definitions of hypnosis as there are books out on the subject. There is one definition, however, I have found most useful. It was given by Dr. William J. Bryan, author of Legal Aspects of Hypnosis (1962), while testifying before the California Assembly's Subcommittee on Professions and Occupations (September 11, 1964). He said: Hypnosis is a state of mind; it is a state in which three things are always present: 1. Superconcentration of the mind. 2. Relaxation of the body, and 3. Increased susceptibility to suggestion. It is important that hypnosis be looked upon as a state of mind. Too many people still adhere to the lingering prejudice; a prejudice born of ignorance that hypnosis is some sort of black magic. It is, of course, neither black nor white magic. But, as long as the misconception persists, the fact that hypnosis is simply a state of mind should be emphasized to add precision and sobriety to any discussion of the subject.

Hypnosis has also been defined as exaggerated suggestibility. This is another good way to understand the term, for in this book proper hypnotic suggestions are considered a key element to one's maximizing his full athletic potential. The alleged drawback to self-hypnosis is that the person, acting as his own hypnotist, might give himself foolish suggestions. This thought is of more theoretical than practical interest. One would not, for example, give himself the suggestion to "go out and play 30 hard sets of tennis without a break." But, just in case you might be such a person, please keep this in mind: self- hypnosis predominately strengthens the mental side of your game. It cannot make you a physical superman; it cannot make you something you are not. **What self-hypnosis does is help you develop and tap your full athletic potential (which might prove to be greater than even you suspect).** To ask more from self-hypnosis, though, is asking too much. So, to sum up, use discretion when you put self-hypnosis to work for you; if you do this, the results should please you immensely. Mastery of self-hypnosis can be of great utility to the serious athlete. It is free, and not dependent upon another person; the hypnotist, who is usually unavailable when you most need him (which is right before or during the competition). By knowing self-hypnosis, you can adapt to changing circumstances during the competition. You are able to do this by giving yourself appropriate hypnotic suggestions as the situation warrants. With additional practice you can give yourself suggestions instantly and without attracting any attention whatsoever. Your opponent and the crowd will not notice anything unusual, because everything will be going on inside your head. By utilizing this instant self-hypnosis capability, you should substantially improve your winning percentage and/or athletic performances. Miroslav Vanek and Bryant Cratty, in Psychology and the Superior Athlete (1970), contend that "hypnosis does not permit an athlete to modify his exertions to an unexpected situation that may confront him, for example, the challenge of an opponent in a race." This contention is technically correct if by "hypnosis" Vanek and Cratty mean "reliance on a hypnotist." The statement is false, though, in cases involving the dexterous application of self-hypnosis. The athlete can use self-hypnosis to modify his exertions as the situation demands if: 1) he is proficient at self-hypnosis, being able to enter the hypnotic state of mind instantly while competing; and/or 2) he performs during the whole competition in the autohypnotic state. In both cases the athlete can immediately give himself appropriate hypnotic suggestions to deal with unforeseen events. The experiences of various elite level athletes, presented throughout this book, will demonstrate that these two capabilities; mastery of instant self-hypnosis, and competing while under self-hypnosis are not impossible to attain. Diligent practice is all that is required.

Why Self-hypnosis and Related Mental Disciplines Work

The human mind, while in a normal waking, or conscious, state, generates what are called Beta waves. These Beta waves, as they show up on an EEG (electroencephalograph) machine, appear as small, compressed, and quite rapid up-and-down lines .Such lines represent a constant flow of energy permeating the brain. Many authorities contend it is the presence of this constant energy level in an awake person's brain which makes self- programming ; that is, convincing oneself to engage in a new behavior or outlook , difficult; simply explained, Beta waves, with their compactness, do not pull apart easily, and so do not readily permit the insertion of different thought patterns. As one goes to sleep, however, or enters into an altered state of consciousness, such as that experienced in hypnosis, the brain wave levels change. Alpha waves or, in even "deeper" states, Theta waves, arise ; waves the EEG machine reveals as being slower, more spaced apart, and possessing greater energy level fluctuations than Beta waves. When these capacious waves prevail in the brain, hypnotic suggestions and their kin are less likely to be shoved out and rejected by the mind; instead, they are more apt to "fit in" and in the process help create a new mind-set. Most coaches are unaware of the Beta to Alpha wave phenomenon and its implications, and continue to resort to old-fashioned "pep talk" sessions in the hope of squeezing better performances out of each athlete. Such sessions, though, are often exercises in futility; not necessarily because advice given by the coach is bad, but rather because the athlete's mind is relatively unreceptive to any new programming. As is the case in one who is awake and attentive; Beta waves predominate in the athlete's brain. And it is at this point where frustration and disenchantment between coach and athlete many times originate. The coach might tell the athlete to do X, but the athlete does Y instead, or tries to do X but fails miserably; this is followed by accusations of insubordination or incompetency, leaving a residue of ill will. Without dwelling upon this matter further, it is important here to observe that there is a big difference between an athlete who is attentive and one who is receptive. The former listens alertly to the message, but often does not act in accordance with it, whereas the latter generally follows the advice with few deviations. Briefly stated, the presence or absence of Beta or Alpha wave levels within the athlete's brain during a coaching input session can contribute to this difference in behavior.

How to Learn Self-hypnosis

Everyone who has explored self-hypnosis has his own preference in reaching the hypnotic state of mind. The following procedure has worked well for the several athletes I have guided toward proficiency in self-hypnosis. Its merit can be attributed to its simplicity.

1. Select a quiet, comfortable place; bed, sofa, soft grass at a park, or whatever. Lie or sit. Remember, a relaxation of the body is necessary, as well as super-concentration of the mind.

2. Keeping your eyes open, find a spot at which to stare. A spot on the ceiling, a leaf in a tree, something of the sort, will do fine. Stare at the spot while mentally telling yourself to relax. Think yourself into relaxation in your own words (whatever words seem to work best for you). Keep staring at the spot all the while. This focus of attention, combined with the command to relax, causes an inhibition effect in the cerebral cortex (the part of the brain concerned with complex mental processes), allowing you to enter the hypnotic state of mind. It is wise to tell yourself to relax once every 20 or 30 seconds. There is no hurry. Instructions given at machine gun rate, however, are not conducive to relaxation. Assuming you are in a reclined position, you will know you are relaxing when your lower back feels as if it is sinking into that on which you are resting. This will be a different, but pleasant, feeling because many athletes, through overdevelopment of their hamstrings and calf muscles, are swayback. (Spend about 5 minutes on this relaxation stage.) 3. By now, your eyes will probably feel tired and want to shut. Go ahead and let them shut. Still talk relaxation to yourself. After another minute, tell yourself: "On the count of three, I will slowly open my eyes. One ... two . . . three." Most likely you will then slowly open your eyes. Keep them open for 20 or 30 seconds. Then tell yourself: "On the count of three, I will slowly close my eyes. One . . . Two . . . three." And, odds are you will slowly close your eyes. (Keep practicing this eye opening and closing drill for about 5 minutes.)
3. If you are not successful with the eye opening and closing drill the first time, keep thinking relaxation, and try again and again if necessary. It is quite easy, really. Spending a few extra moments to master this drill is well worth it! Having succeeded at the eye opening and closing drill, congratulations are in order, for most assuredly you have attained the hypnotic state of mind. It is not necessary to attempt any further drills to "prove" you are under hypnosis. You could try a different drill, as occasionally do the athletes with whom I have worked, whereby you practice folding and unfolding your hands across your stomach.
4. But, you do not need to do this. The mastery of the eye opening and closing drill does not constitute, of course, the deepest stage of hypnosis; it is a state, though, that will respond favorably to hypnotic suggestions.
5. You do not have to be "real deep" to successfully program into your subconscious the hypnotic suggestions you give yourself. The hypnotic stage represented by control over small muscle groups such as the eyes is sufficient. 4. "Awake" yourself. (You are not really "asleep" while practicing self-hypnosis; actually, you are very much awake. In fact, if the house started to burn down, you would not keep lying there. You'd get out!) To "awake," simply tell yourself: "On the count of three, I will awake. One . . . two . . . three. I'm awake!" After saying this, you will probably look around, slowly sit up, and generally puzzle over the experience through which you have just been. This is a common reaction. The first session at learning self-hypnosis is an out-of-the-ordinary happening.

6. So, you should be puzzled afterwards, especially if you did not believe in hypnosis or thought you could not be hypnotized. 5. Now that you are "awake" again, you should attempt to put yourself back in the hypnotic state. This is done to make sure you have learned self-hypnosis. To reenter the hypnotic state, you do not need to repeat the entire routine (which you already know works). Perhaps just close your eyes and talk relaxation for a minute. However you go about it, you know you are succeeding when these sensations typical of hypnosis come over you: 1) a detached feeling, 2) a heaviness or numbness in your arms and legs, and 3) a disinclination to exert yourself and move about. At this stage you may still be unsure that you have reattained the hypnotic state. If this is the case, it is all right to try, for example, the eye opening and closing drill. By the third or fourth self- hypnosis session, though, you should be able to dispense with such proofs and reassurances. Progress comes fast when you practice. "Reawaken" yourself after regaining the hypnotic state of mind. It should be emphasized that you should have no trouble reawakening yourself. As Dr. Kroger observes, "Failures in self- dehypnotization are rare," adding that he personally "has never had a case."

7. Summary of First Self-hypnosis Session

The steps you can follow during your first self-hypnosis session can be summarized as: 1. Lie or sit in a quiet, comfortable place. 2. Stare at a point while telling yourself to relax. (Spend about 5 minutes.) 3. Allow your eyes to close. Then, give yourself the suggestion to open them. After your eyes open, give yourself the suggestion to close them. Keep repeating this process. (Spend about 5 minutes.) 4. "Awake" yourself. ("On the count of three, I will awaken. One... two... three. I'm awake! ") 5. Put yourself back in the hypnotic state. Once you succeed, "reawaken" yourself. It is important that you practice self-hypnosis as much as possible, for that is how you become proficient at the technique.

"Autohypnosis," informs Dr. Kroger, "is a learned conditioned response; therefore, one must try to practice as much as possible every day."

How long should these practice sessions last, and how many should you do? Dr. Kroger suggests one perform "half a dozen sessions of 2 or 10 minutes each throughout the day," these being "more practical than lengthier sessions." Dr. Kroger's recommendation to practice self-hypnosis frequently while keeping the sessions short is one well-suited for athletes. As an athlete, you desire the capability of entering and exiting the hypnotic state as quickly as possible. During competitions you usually do not have much time to collect your thoughts for the unexpected situations that often develop. So, you want to be able to give yourself appropriate hypnotic suggestions, if needed, during a time out or some break in the action.

The 2-minute self-hypnosis practice session Dr. Kroger recommends is a good simulation, therefore, of an emergency self-hypnosis session you might wish to conduct during a short break in the competition. Of course, if you practice self-hypnosis diligently, you can also develop the advanced capability of entering the hypnotic state during the actual competition, and give yourself suggestions on the spot. As I have indicated, speed of entering the hypnotic state of mind is primarily a function of practice. The more you practice self-hypnosis, the faster you will be able to enter the hypnotic state, give yourself suggestions, and respond to those suggestions. But, even if you do not develop the ideal; the instant self-hypnosis capability, you can still use self-hypnosis to gain an enormous mental edge over your opponent. As the old saying by Voltaire goes, "Best is the enemy of the good enough." Knowing and faithfully applying self-hypnosis to your sports is good enough; good enough to improve your athletic performance substantially. Acquiring the self-hypnosis capability, and employing it in areas of your life where you desire success, such as your sports, will place you head and shoulders above the crowd. For the crowd will not make the effort to learn self-hypnosis; they are too busy getting drunk or whatever, and do not care about self-improvement. Remember: You don't have to be best at something if you are the only one who's trying it at all!

Hypnotic Suggestions

The purpose of getting into the autohypnotic state is to give you hypnotic suggestions. It is the suggestions which allow you to overcome all those mental obstacles that often prevent you from achieving your full athletic potential. Let me present a hypothetical example showing how hypnotic suggestions can help you. (The outcome of this example is not so hypothetical when we examine the numerous success stories appearing later in this book; instead, it is a matter of course.) You are a tennis player. You have a match lined up in the afternoon against an old-time rival of yours. Your matches are usually close. You know exactly what you have to do to win. Unfortunately, you have not been winning recently. Desiring therefore to end the frustrating losing streak, you put yourself in the hypnotic state, and give yourself the suggestions to "swing through on the backhand" and "play your game." So, what happens? Your opponent plays his usual good game, but, somewhat surprisingly, you prevail. And wonder of wonders: you swung through on every backhand; something you have not done in months! Skeptics would pass this incident off as coincidence. Meanwhile, you might simply say, "Well, I finally put it together." While your statement contains more factuality than the skeptics' claim of coincidence, it is not too enlightening. In reality, the hypnotic suggestions to "swing through on the backhand" and "play your game" brought out the best in you, which made it possible for you to win the match.

Realize this: hypnotic suggestions act on the subconscious; that great stock of knowledge which, while often forgotten and submerged, is capable of being recalled. This means that, in our example of the frustrated tennis player, you resurrect all those astonishing shots that once upon a time carried you to glory; topspin backhands, swinging volleys, and the like. Keep in mind that the degree to which hypnotic suggestions can help you implement good tennis shots, or whatever, depends upon the current state of your athletic potential. If you are out of practice and not in the best physical condition, obviously your athletic potential is not as great as it could be. It limits the extent to which you can be helped by hypnotic suggestions. Another important point to know is that hypnotic suggestions possess an impelling force. It is as if you must carry out the suggestions. It would not be unusual if you did not carry out the suggestions; nothing is foolproof. But, it would be most unlikely. By giving yourself appropriate hypnotic suggestions, you should perform well despite the strongest efforts of your conscious self to make you do otherwise. You will do well because, essentially, your subconscious is in charge. The hypnotic suggestions will not work as intended all the time; they cannot guarantee victory or super performances; but, assuming you persist in practicing self-hypnosis, the suggestions will work often enough and impressively enough for you to notice a substantial improvement in your athletic performance and won/loss record. As Dr. Kroger observes of self-hypnosis, it **"makes available a tremendous reservoir of unrecognized potential strength"** the "forgotten assets." Diligent practice, however, generally is necessary for this to occur.

Types of Suggestions

Athletes new to self-hypnosis often wonder what types of hypnotic suggestions they should give themselves. The choice is between suggestions of a general nature or those of a technical, specific nature. A general suggestion would be "I will concentrate on every point" or "I will play as hard as I can, and win!" In contrast, a technical suggestion might be "I will keep my arms up on defense" or "I will step into the volley." Both types of suggestions are valuable. Which type is more valuable for you depends upon your own particular needs.

Personally, I prefer general suggestions. **When you give yourself a general suggestion, such as "play hard and win," the technical matters tend to take care of themselves.** Also, you can lose sight of your overall objective if you emphasize technical suggestions. The bottom line, which is to improve your athletic performance and/or to win, is top priority. Take care of it first; then, if you want, you can concern yourself with technical matters. Emil Coue, an eminent hypnotist of the early 1900s, also advocated general suggestions. To him the end result was the only thing that counted. Dr. Kroger relates that Coue emphasized that a general, nonspecific suggestion was best, since it would be received uncritically. He became famous for a phrase he urged his patients to say to themselves several times a day,

'Everyday, in every way, I am getting better and better. Note that Coue's phrase does not enter into details about how the person will get better and better; just that he will. Does the phrase work, though? In many instances, yes. Coue enjoyed enormous success with his patients, who responded most favorably to the general autosuggestions they gave themselves. This was no accident, for clinical studies by psychiatrist John Hartland and associates of his confirm the effectiveness of the general autosuggestion approach. From this it should follow that what works for people in the area of health most certainly will work for them in the area of sports.

When to Give Yourself Suggestions

Probably the most convenient time to give yourself autosuggestions is on the same day you compete. Obviously, you do this minutes or hours before the competition begins. By waiting until the day you compete: 1) you should know who your opponent will be, and perhaps have a chance to gather intelligence about his strengths and weaknesses, and 2) you should know what the weather will be like, whether or not you will be playing before a hostile crowd; in short, better understand the playing conditions that might affect your performance. Knowing these variables, you will be able to give yourself tailor-made autosuggestions. For example, if you know the crowd will be against you, you can give yourself the suggestion, "During the entire game I will play with total concentration no matter what!"
This kind of suggestion will go a long way toward eliminating the crowd as a factor. Another excellent reason to give yourself autosuggestions on the same day on which you compete is that the suggestions will be fresh. Studies indicate that the more recent the auto- suggestion, the more likely it is that you will carry it out completely. Reports Dr. Kroger, posthypnotic suggestion may last for months to years. It is agreed, however, that it may remain effective for several months. During this period, decrement occurs in the quality of the posthypnotic performance. There is nothing wrong with giving yourself autosuggestions a couple of weeks or months before a big game or match; in fact, it is highly commendable that you do this. To be on the safe side, though, give yourself reinforcing autosuggestions on the day of competition. You want to do this in case the effects of your earlier suggestions have waned. Ideally, for a major upcoming competition, you should give yourself autosuggestions every day in the days or weeks preceding the contest, as well as on the day you perform. If you do this, about the only way you can lose is if your opponent is physically and/or technically superior to you. (You try to be sure that such is not the case by working on your physical fitness and the technical aspects required in your sport.) Some people believe constant reinforcement will render autosuggestion "stale" and ineffective; actually, the opposite is true. Dr. Kroger notes: "Periodic reinforcement tends to increase its effectiveness; repeated elicitation does not weaken it." Therefore one should not worry about too much reinforcement.

So, the answer to the question, "When do you give yourself autosuggestions?" is (1) especially on the day you compete, and (2) preferably on the days and weeks preceding the competition as well.

Giving Yourself Autosuggestions during Competition without Anyone Noticing

Having developed the ability to instantly enter and exit the hypnotic state, you quickly can give yourself suggestions and "awaken" yourself, thereby wrapping up the session without making it some sort of grand production. I have also mentioned that you can develop the capability of playing your sport while in the hypnotic state (this is something I have done occasionally). By giving yourself the suggestion to "act normal but still remain under hypnosis," you can compete in your sport; carry on a conversation, and so on without others being the wiser. Perfecting this capability takes a little extra practice, and one's first attempt sometimes betrays a lack of spontaneity and monotone- sounding speech. In any event, competing while in the hypnotic state has no great advantage over giving yourself autosuggestions beforehand, and during breaks and time outs. But, you wonder, how can I give myself suggestions during breaks and time outs? Obviously, quickness, developed from practice, is the key. And quickness is imperative because the rules do not permit you much time during breaks and time outs. In a tennis match, for example, you are allowed but one minute to rest and towel off between the changes of sides. So, to use self-hypnosis during competition you must be able to rapidly enter the hypnotic state, give yourself suggestions, and "awaken" yourself; all this must take place in a minute or less. Once again, though, this capability is not that difficult to develop. Many athletes acquire the necessary speed after just a couple of self-hypnosis practice sessions. By giving yourself autosuggestions quickly, you escape attention and do not attract stares. This is an important point because most of us are self-conscious to some degree. Your opponent and the spectators really will not look at you twice as you sit on the bench during a break with your eyes closed (or however else you appear while giving yourself autosuggestions). At most they will say, "Oh, he's resting" or "He's concentrating." Even if there is an expert on self- hypnosis in the crowd, he will not know for sure what you are doing. He would have to ask you afterwards if you were using self-hypnosis or meditation during the breaks to confirm his suspicions. Despite outward appearances, you are not "resting" or merely "concentrating." Through self-hypnosis you are actually laying the groundwork for your victory and your opponent's downfall. Of course, your opponent does not know that. In fact, afterwards he will probably wonder what hit him, what kind of dynamo he just ran up against. Sometimes your opponent or the spectators will be too gregarious. During breaks you might be unable to give yourself autosuggestions because of people, or your opponent, talking to you; or, some other interruptions might arise. There is little you can do about this. Just make sure that before you arrive for the competition you have already given yourself suggestions.

Summary of Important Points

To become proficient in the use of self-hypnosis, and also a mentally tough athlete: 1) Practice self-hypnosis as often as possible. Spend 2 to 10 minutes for each practice session. Attempt to acquire the instant self-hypnosis capability. 2) Give yourself general autosuggestions ("I will play with total confidence and win!"). Do this first. Then, if necessary, you can also employ technical suggestions. 3) Give yourself suggestions every day in the days or weeks before the competition, because reinforcement makes the suggestions more effective. Definitely give yourself suggestions on the day you compete. 4) If the situation requires, reenter the hypnotic state and reinforce your suggestions during a break or time out. Your opponent and the spectators will simply think you are "resting" or "concentrating." By following these steps, you can achieve your full athletic potential. You will put pressure on your opponent. He will have to perform really well because you will not beat yourself through mental errors and "choking."

Music as an aid

(Starting paragraph is referencing Tennis great Billie Jean King)

Telling yourself "to win" provides a drive, a killer instinct; something so many players lack. And there is nothing wrong with giving yourself this suggestion. After all, your opponent will gladly close out the match on you given the opportunity; so, return the favor.) King's interest in mental training strategies is apparently not limited to self-hypnosis. According to teaching pro Bill Sheen, King also used a "stress tape" he has put out. Virginia Wade, 1977 Wimbledon champion, is supposed to have regularly listened to the tape, too, which makes sense because Sheen says she gave him the idea. The 22-minute cassette contains classical music, its purpose being to reduce tension. L. A. Time's staff writer John Weyler decided to look into the matter. He interviewed Sheen, who revealed how the tape's music seems to benefit one along both physical and mental lines: "We did biofeedback tests with scans on the heart, body temperature and the brain," he said. "The results showed the music reduced the heart rate and body temperature and had a profound effect on the hypothalamus section of the brain, which controls the secretions of hormones from the pituitary. . ." "Most players tell me about a change in attitude," Sheen said. "The music tends to make one introspective and people become more aware of themselves. What often results is a more positive attitude." [8] Sheen's classical music "stress tape," which really should be called an anti-stress tape, is hardly a breakthrough idea.

Champion weight lifter Russ Knipp, for example, said in 1977 that the Bulgarian Olympic lifters "**use music as one form of concentration**" (see Weightlifting chapter). In fact, music therapy has for some time been widely practiced throughout Europe. Even 800 years ago, the great Jewish physician Moses Maimonides, in his treatise On the Causes of Symptoms, written for his patron, Sultan Saladin of Egypt, advised the Sultan to lie down after eating breakfast, while "the chanter should intone with the strings and raise his voice and continue his melodies for an hour. Then, the chanter should lower his voice gradually, loosen his strings and soften his melody until he (the Sultan) sleeps deeply, whereupon he should stop." Added Maimonides, "Physicians and philosophers have already mentioned that sleep in this manner, when the melody of the strings induces sleep, endows the psyche with good nature and dilates it greatly, improving its management of the body." You might wish to experiment on your own with soft classical music. It is not difficult to concoct your own anti-stress tape; but, if you want to avoid the effort, there is always Sheen's tape and others like it; still a good investment. No matter what you decide, it certainly would not hurt to incorporate calming music into the time you set aside for mental preparation for your upcoming competition or workout. Besides this, you may be wise to listen to such music during other periods of the day, for more and more evidence suggests that the employment of anti-stress measures is indispensable for survival in Western society.

More on Stress

According to Dr. James Skinner, a Baylor University neurophysiologist, stress is what usually causes heart attacks, not clogged arteries. We note this pertinent section in the November 10, 1978 L. A. Time's article, "Stress Alone Can Kill, Expert Says": Skinner said his Houston laboratory blocked the coronary arteries of a group of pigs, the animal whose cardiovascular system most resembles man's. Some of them had been subjected to physical and psychological stress, such as being placed in unfamiliar surroundings or receiving mild electric shocks to the skin. The stressed animals died within a matter of minutes. The animals not under stress did not die, even when the major blood supply to their hearts was blocked. Explained Dr. Skinner, "We found that the psychological factor was necessary for the occlusion (blockage) of the coronary artery to produce ventricular fibrillation, the death-causing component of heart attacks." As Dr. Skinner further observed, "it may be that brain states alone" Tennis 23 are what triggers heart attacks. If so, this would help explain the puzzling circumstance of heart attacks striking people regarded to be in excellent physical condition. The pressures of modern society being what they are, Dr. Skinner suggests that science develop an "anti-stress pill" to help people deal with the situation. But, this development has already occurred. We can easily get through the day by utilizing meditation, calming music, and other proven stress combaters such as proper nutrition and daily exercise; such strategies as these make up the "anti-stress pill."

All this is necessary to bring up because even some top athletes, presumably in peak physical condition, have suffered heart attacks. In tennis the most famous example is that of Arthur Ashe, who incurred a heart attack in early August, 1979, and underwent a quadruple heart by-pass operation the following December. One wonders if by 1979 Ashe had abandoned the meditation- like procedure he had used at Wimbledon in 1975. Whatever the case, meditation offers one approach toward reducing stress. Studies by Dr. Ronald Jenning and Dr. Archie Wilson, professors of medicine at the University of California, Irvine, verify this. Scott Moore, L.A. Times staff writer, reported that one study by Dr. Jenning and Dr. Wilson "indicated that those who practice meditation experience a decrease in the hormone Cortisol, an indicator of stress in their blood flow during meditation. Another study showed a decrease in blood lactate concentrations, another stress indicator, during meditation. Such studies are cause for optimism. They demonstrate that once we become aware of the stress factors present in our lives, we can do something to reduce or eliminate their negative impact.

The book goes into great detail for using the mental techniques described above, with more specific tips and examples for a number of sports. I just wanted to share some of the more general highlights of the book, as I think there are some great points contained there.

Here is a little something about training the will, which I think goes hand in hand with the ideas we have been looking at already;

THE TRAINING OF THE WILL
By ROBERTO ASSAGIOLI, M.D.

INTRODUCTION—THE NEED TO TRAIN THE WILL

The wide gulf between the external and inner powers of modern man is the most important and profound cause of the individual and collective evils which hinder the progress and even menace the future of our civilization. Modern man has paid dearly for the external powers and advantages he has gained; while his life is richer, broader and more intense, it is at the same time much more complicated and exhausting.

Its rapidly increasing pace, the countless enticements it offers, the complicated economic and social machinery in which it has enmeshed him, make ever increasing and more insistent demands upon his nervous energy, his mental powers, his emotions and his will. To realize this, one has only to observe the day's work of an active business man, scientist or prominent politician, the daily round of a leading society woman, of an actress, or of a housewife with a large family. Frequently the individual has not the resources to cope with the hard necessities, to resist the enticements or to avoid the many pitfalls of such a life. Nervous equilibrium is destroyed, the person is overwhelmed by despondency and a sense of frustration and even despair, and he allows himself to be mastered by his lower drives. In order to remedy these evils, to eliminate this lack of balance between the outer and the inner powers of man, two generally applicable methods can be used. One is *simplification of the external life*; the other is the *development of the inner powers*. Everyone can resist, at least to some extent, the attractions of the world and the rush of modern life can
eliminate some of its unnecessary complications, re-establish a closer contact with nature, and learn to relax and rest at intervals. However, this first method is in itself insufficient and in many cases difficult to apply. Duties of every kind, family ties, professional obligations, etc., keep us bound to the wheel of modern life and often compel us to participate in its hurried pace. Very few of us possess the will power to resist the general current. Moreover, modern man would certainly not give up the powers over nature which he has acquired, and it would not be desirable for him to do so. The evil does not lie in the powers themselves but in the use man makes of them and in the fact that he allows them to overcome him and make him their slave. It is necessary for the sanity, happiness and dignity of modern man that he should develop his inner powers with the same intense desire and concentration that he now devotes towards external achievements. The very pivot of all development of the inner powers is the training of the Will. St. Augustine, with one of his concise and apt expressions, said, "Homines sunt voluntates" (men are wills). Indeed, it is the will that constitutes the real innermost center of man; it is that which makes him truly himself. Without it, the ablest and most intelligent individual would be no more than an ingenious automaton. The man of weak will is like a cork on the ocean, tossed by every wave; or like the weather vane, turned about by every gust of wind. He is the slave not only of the will of others and all external circumstances, but also of his drives and desires. He is unable to make adequate use of his talents and aptitudes; he is unable to live up to his convictions. On the other hand, the man who has developed a strong and steady will finds his rightful position in the world by overcoming all obstacles, both those created by circumstances and those due to his own weaknesses or urges. Thus he acquires the power to reach the goals he has chosen; in other words, he succeeds, and also gains that which is better than worldly success: the satisfaction of having attained his ends through his own efforts, by means of his will, and the assurance of having within himself the power to fight and to win again and again, if necessary. Such a man has eliminated from his consciousness one of the most common causes of unhappiness and failure—that is, fear. He has learned to face life with resolute and steadfast confidence and say to it: "I know thee and I fear thee not."

But it is not enough that the will should be merely strong; such a will is liable to errors and excesses which may lead the individual astray and bring about dangerous reactions. There are psychological laws as exact and certain as natural laws, and their neglect or violation brings inevitable and often severe punishment. Thus we frequently see people of strong will misusing their precious instrument by violent clashes or exaggerated efforts; they use methods which are too harsh and aggressive, resulting in inner and external conflicts and in nervous and psychological troubles. Instead, by using more skilful and harmonious ways, based on a sound knowledge of the constitution and functioning of the psyche, they could make headway more easily; they could handle the opposing forces so as to utilize them constructively, thus attaining the desired ends with a minimum of effort. But even when the will is endowed with both strength and skill, it is not yet a complete will, nor is it always helpful; it may even be a very harmful weapon, for if such a will is directed, consciously or unconsciously, towards evil ends, it becomes a real danger to society. A man of strong and able will, capable of using his natural gifts to the utmost, can overpower and corrupt the will of others; one who dares everything, fears nothing, and whose actions are not restrained by any moral law, by any sense of love and compassion, can have a disastrous influence on a community or on an entire nation. There are also moral and spiritual laws which are no less strict and inviolable than the physical and psychological laws, although their action is more subtle and less obvious. The great law of action and reaction, of rhythm and equilibrium, which operates in the natural world is just as powerful in the moral and spiritual spheres. Those who do evil attract evil upon themselves, those who are violent and merciless ultimately provoke the violence and cruelty of others against themselves. History offers many such examples from Caligula to Rasputin and to Hitler. Therefore it is necessary, both for the general welfare and our own, that our will should be *good*, as well as strong and skilful. Only this is the true, the *whole* will; only such a will can give us both practical success and the highest inner satisfaction. In it lies one of the secrets of the great men and women whom we admire and revere. The question now arises: Is it possible to form and develop a will of this kind? How should one set about such a task? And by what means can it be accomplished? It is possible to develop such a will; the past and the presentgive us many examples of men and women who have achieved it. The means to this end do exist and have always been more or less known and used. In recent times much progress has been made in this respect: the investigation of the less known facts and the laws of human psychology, of the various manifestations of the emotions and of the powers latent in the self, has been undertaken and actively carried on. The will is often confused with strong drives, with obstinacy, with impulse, with intense outward activity. It is a common thing to consider and admire, as persons endowed with a strong will, the business man who, from small beginnings, has built up a fortune; the stern and authoritative general; the explorer who faces dangers and discomforts. It is, however, quite possible that all these do not really possess a strong will and that they may be "possessed" by a drive, such as greed for money, ambition, the thirst for sensation or the glamour of adventure. In order to know what the will really is, we must discover it in ourselves. It is an inner condition difficult to describe or define. It is one of those fundamental experiences which cannot actually be communicated by means of words, but which must be lived individually.

Who could explain what the sense of beauty consists of, and how it is kindled in human beings? It is a "revelation", an "awakening", which may come to a man as he looks at a glorious sunset, a majestic glacier or into the clear and innocent eyes of a child; it may arise while contemplating "The Last Supper" of Leonardo da Vinci or Michelangelo's "David"; while reading one of the literary masterpieces or listening to the celestial harmonies of Wagner's "Parsifal". This awakening sense of the beautiful, confused at first, becomes clearer and more developed through repeated experiences of an aesthetic kind, and is also cultivated through the study of aesthetics and the history of art. But no amount of intellectual study can by itself take the place of the initial revelation. On the other hand, while the aesthetic sense cannot be taught, its awakening can be facilitated and often brought about by creating favorable circumstances for this purpose; for instance, by the quiet and repeated contemplation of natural scenery and works of art, or by opening oneself to the charm of music. The same is true concerning the will. At a given moment, generally in a crisis, we have a vivid and unmistakable inner experience of its reality and nature. In the face of danger, when the instinct of self preservation urges us to take refuge in flight, or when fear threatens to paralyze our limbs, suddenly, from the mysterious depths of our being, there arises an unsuspected energy which enables us to place a firm foot on the edge of the abyss or to confront our aggressor with calmness and resolution. Before the threatening attitude of a superior, or when confronting an excited mob, when every personal reason would induce us to yield, the energy of the will gives us the power to say resolutely: "No! At all costs I stand by my convictions; I shall carry out what I consider to be my duty." Similarly, when we are in the presence of some insinuating and seductive temptation, the energy of the will rises up, shakes us out of our dangerous acquiescence and sets us free from the snare In other cases, the inner experience of "willing' comes to us in a more quiet and subtle way. In times of silence and meditation, in the careful examination of our motives, or in the thoughtful pondering on decisions, there arises within us a "voice", small but distinct, that urges us in a certain direction; a voice different from that of our ordinary motives and impulses. We feel that it comes from the real and central core of our being. Or else, in this inner illumination, we come to realize that the essential note of the spirit is the *Will*, an overwhelming energy that brushes aside every obstacle and asserts itself, irresistible and effective. However, the simplest and most frequent way in which we discover our will lies in determined action and struggle. When we make a physical or mental effort, when we are actively wrestling with some obstacle or opposing forces, we feel a specific power rising up within us; we become animated by an inner energy and experience a sense of "willing'. In these last cases, however, this is rarely the pure and unalloyed will, since our action is not determined only by a direct act of the will, but also by a multiplicity of desires, hopes, fears, needs, drives. It is well to realize thoroughly the full meaning and the immense value of the discovery of the will. In whatever way it happens, either spontaneously or through conscious action, in a crisis or in the quiet of inner recollection, it constitutes a most important and decisive event in our lives. The will is the central power of our individuality, the innermost essence of us; therefore, in a certain sense, the discovery of the will means the discovery of our true being.

The article from which this was excerpted goes on to describe a number of exercises that are designed to train the will, but I will not go into these as I think the methods of self-hypnosis, visualization and the related disciplines are superior to these suggestions.

I thought it would make a good addition to the book to get inputs from some well known folks in the iron game, "straight from the horse's mouth" so to speak. I asked everybody the same set of questions; shown below:

In your training and competition, how do you prepare yourself mentally for the challenges? Have you ever tried self hypnosis or hired an actual hypnotist for training? Do you or have you ever used visualization techniques? How important would you say attitude/mental focus is to strength training? In your vast experience in the game, can you relate some stories about how some of the greats you have witnessed got "jacked up" or otherwise mentally prepared to make a big lift?

The responses were as follow;

Richard Sorin's response:

Richard Sorin

Richard Sorin (Soar-in)
Nicknames: Pops aka Dops aka Gripasaurus aka Mr. Richard

Age: 59
Height: 6' 5"
Bodyweight: 270 lbs

Athletic experience:

- High school All-American in track
- College letter in track all 4 years
- Masters All-American track (Discus)
- Masters National Champion powerlifting
- South Carolina masters state record holder in powerlifting
- South Carolina record holder in Olympic weightlifting
- 45 years coaching experience in track, Olympic lifting, and Powerlifting
- First to close #3 gripper.

Lifting Style (Current):

- Powerlifting movements
- Olympic weightlifting movements
- Power bodybuilding movements
- Grip training

POWER PEOPLE

Richard Sorin, President of Sorin Exercise Equipment of Irmo, South Carolina, is the only known man in the world who can close the #3 Silver Crush TM Gripper sold by IronMind Enterprises. According to Randall J. Strossen, Ph.D., President of IronMind Enterprises, the list of people who have tried the #3 gripper and failed reads like a Who's Who of Olympic and Powerlifting. Rich can also do 35 consecutive reps with the #2 gripper. At age 41, he has pulled up a 675 lb. deadlift in the 275. (photo courtesy Strossen).

Area(s) of Expertise:

- Throwing shot-put
- Discus
- Olympic weightlifting
- Powerlifting

- Strength training for athletics

What got you into weight training / what is your training past:
Brought my first barbell set in to show-and-tell at age 5 (55 years ago)

Current Goals:

- Compete in track and field and Olympic weightlifting in age group competition.
- Increased cardio training integrated with strength training.
- Shutting the #3 gripper at age 60.

Performance PR's

Bench - 470lbs

Squat - 675lbs

Dead - 714lbs

Clean - 410lbs

Snatch - 290lbs

Any other thing you want to mention:
A thought...One lion can only do so much, a pride of lions can conquer anything.

Dave, Well here a few personal views on training and competition.

Q,1. How important would you say attitude/ mental focus is to strength training?
A,1 strength training and power sports involve high levels of not only muscle recruitment but high levels of excitability from the nervous and endocrine systems. General high levels of focused mental awareness of the battle to follow must be kept close at hand but with a very strong on off switch coupled with an easily regulated throttle. Success in strength is made with mental focus first to the task

but also the attention to detail coupled with a level of resolve that is perceived by others. If they see that look on your face that you are fully prepared to go to a place they can never follow, you will prevail. When others get to believe this THEY decide then that they can't beat you.

Q,2 Did you ever use visualization techniques?
A,2 Yes from a very early age I would use mental visualization. First of all deciding long before I touched a weight what my goals for the day were and actually HOW the particular lifts would look. If it was a big or record weight I would visualize enough so there was no doubt on the lift because I had truly completed it once in my mind.
It is easy for the body to follow doing a task after it has already been done. I would pause briefly before actual attempts seeing the entire lift being successfully done in my mind. I would never touch the bar until all doubt or fear was gone.

Q,3 have I ever tried self hypnosis?
A,3 Yes !!!. A great measure of my success in grip , Olympic ,and power lifting was to be able to literally convince myself short of dying there was no way I would give up or back down. Total commitment or nothing. When reaching that zone I developed a method of actually focusing strength into a particular area(like a tree putting all.it's energy into one leaf) while being able at a seconds notice to create a huge adrenalin dump into my involved body parts. A feeling like an instant life or death situation but self imposed...at will. Pain, stress, and effort are blocked out into an automatic almost numbed feeling. Although hypnotized before and strong minded I never have sought out a hypnotist for training. The hypnotist I did use was actually a dentist. As I sit writing this within a seconds pause I can close my eyes and bring that tingling power felt in my body , perhaps available from a half century of practice.

Q,4 How did you prepare for training and contests mentally?
A,4 I was always easily excitable by nature so it blended well into competitive situations. Staying on high alert always burns energy, makes you move slower and not be able to gather for that one all out moment. If anything more than competition is needed to focus I have never used it. Caffeine, stimulants, slapping, etc, or not being able to apply instant rage then disarm is waste in my opinion. As a meet became closer my level of awareness and urgency to a task narrows until that final moment. To fine hone that on/ off switch is the key...do not waste "it"
Q,5 In your experience in the game can you relate some stories of the greats and how they got "jacked up" preparing for a big lift?

A, 5 I have had the pleasure to see some world shaking lifts in my day by distinctly varied individuals. All were great, all were gifted, all were able to use and focus more of their gift in an effective way than their peers. I will mention three briefly, all greats, but upon my personal on site observations got the mental battle won in different ways.

The first **Donnie Thompson;** holder of the highest powerlifting total of all time, He was focused on Donnie and what it took to maintain him until his meet. His mind was bubbling but not boiling. Eating, resting, lowering stress and selecting numbers to start with were his agenda. He was deliberate, quiet and relied on the support of his team to provide external fire. He knew what he needed to do and could do. No yelling, stomping , slapping or outward show of rage as he revved up that bulldozer like power. Deliberate, and polished. All cards were hidden. The plan long in motion was completed.

The second person up the level was Bob Bednarski one of the brightest stars ever on the Olympic weightlifting platform. What a switch he had! Total calm before the storm, lying about as if eating grapes on the royal barge. As he stepped on the platform, he was still calm, but focused . As his hands rose over his head in his signature manner the switch turned on to total animal power! His lifts were so intense, even violent, it was like a train wreck fed by the crowd. The lift (446 world record clean and jerk) was so overwhelming I greeted him as he leaped off the stage (I was barely 16) his whole body was still shaking from the mighty effort.

In the midst of signing the papers for a world record and the weight being officially weighed he "turned off the switch "in a moment of kindness and said" hey let's take a picture over hear near those plants, they look nice". We left the crowd and calmly walked across the entire gym for a friendly picture. That really blew my mind. A total on, a total off switch!

My last athlete to contrast was Bill Kazmier during his peak at the 1981 World's Strongest Man contest which although injured, won. Bill was possessed, and a phenomenal athlete. He was in a total, contorted rage in the hours leading up to the contest, removed and like a huge storm ever building as he gathered for the effort.

There was no approaching him knowing from respect" he needed the time". The look of rage in his eyes and the formidable hulking body threw fear into all the competitors. He was on a mission. Hurt or not he blocked out all pain and truly first convinced himself, then others he was the best of the day before ever touching a weight.
With a torn pec and angered by a disputed referee call he then requested a 100lb more than any competitor had done. With a cruel roll of thunder overhead and a growl he pulled the record 975 for not one, but two reps. Point proved, he then won.

Richard Sorin

And further

Dave,
Many thanks! My son that was a record holder in track and field through college in the 35 lb weight throw and the amateur world highland games champion . He added a pearl of wisdom about super star hammer thrower Yuri Sedykh. While all the Americans were running around yelling and throwing "all out" warm-up throws Yuri sat quietly alone under a tree. When the Americans expended their explosive energy he simply walked up and destroyed his first official throw and present record. The competition just crumbled before his eyes. He said that as a group "they never learned."

From Dr. Squat, Fred Hatfield;

There's an old axiom, "If you can visualize doing it, you can do it." I have found this to be true in sports. To me, visualization is the most important form of practice. Imperceptible neuronal activation both at the motor level and at the cognitive level leave a "footprint" that can be followed in later practice.

CONDITIONING YOUR MIND

Beyond pumping iron there is another kind of preparation for bodybuilding competition, a preparation just as important, and one that involves subtle factors concerning your attitude and mental approach to training and competition. You can achieve great things with your body if you learn how to use your mind. Learning to harness the power of your mind can advance your physical training a giant step further. It can also make the difference between winning and losing in competition. Mind power and success through mind conditioning only comes with a sustained and sincere effort. You can't make a wish and hope that it comes true and forget about working on it. The mind reacts much the same way the body does. If you train and condition it regularly, it responds with great efficiency and effectiveness. On the other hand, if you assume, as so many bodybuilders do, that it's good enough the way it is, your chances of achieving your maximum potential are greatly diminished. If you had foolishly assumed that attitude about your body, you would never have entered the gym to train in the first place. Some of the key ingredients to an effective mind conditioning program are 1) motivation, 2) incentive, 3) visualization, and, most important of all, 4) belief. You've gotta believe. You've gotta believe in yourself, in your talents and capabilities, in your goals and all you hope to achieve, and in your methods for achieving them. The key to understanding what your mind holds in store for you is a simple realization. Realize that within you is all the power you need to succeed both in training and in competition. Within you is all the potential for success. Within you is the brain power of an infinitely superior person, physically, spiritually and mentally. Once you make this realization -- that your mind holds a vast wealth of knowledge, information, control, power, ability and potential -- you can start to tap it. You can delve into your own secret depths and find out what you're really made of.

Here is a simple step-by-step method to getting what you want:

Step 1:
Define your tasks toward perfection clearly and write them down. This means being specific about what you want. You'll be surprised at how much clearer you can make it by simply putting it in words.
Step 2:
Devise a series of logic-based stepping stones toward perfecting your skill.
Step 3:
Create your strategy for success. This is your game plan, your INTEGRATED training program.
Step 4:
Visualize yourself succeeding. You must actually "see" yourself, in your mind's eye, doing exactly what your plan will accomplish.
Step 5:
By affirming your commitment to perfection, and actually visualizing and verbalizing your commitment, you will find that your mind, body, spirit and emotional self all become one. Repeat your commitment statement before, during and after your success visualization every day.
Step 6:
Finally, "anchor" the significance of your achievement firmly in your mind and soul. Self-reward often works.

The key to mental conditioning is to make your new thoughts and new approach a habit. The more regular your new habit becomes, the more quickly old and destructive habits fade away. It usually takes about three weeks to implement this revised way of thinking. During that time you're likely to feel tempted to return to old patterns and habits, feeling that the old way was easier and "good enough."

Don't do it!

From Vince Anello

Dave I believe the mental side is the most important part in success in anything!!! There are hundreds of different methods to achieve anything. The common denominator is mental attitude. I have experimented with many different training methods. What made me succeed; I believe was my mental attitude. That is true with my clients also in sticking to a healthy diet and training. Those clients that achieve the best in fat loss (if that is their goal) are not those that have the best diet but those that have the best attitude!!!! I have studied many different forms of mental training Silva, tm, nlp, self hypnosis and many more.

I thought I should provide at least this snippet on Silva since Vince mentioned it here;

About Jose Silva 1914–1999

Jose Silva is the founder of The Silva Method, and a pioneer in mind empowerment research.

Silva dedicated his life to **awakening the human mind's hidden potential**. After over a decade of research, he released his findings in 1966 and spent the rest of his life perfecting and teaching The Silva Method.

Silva's legacy is carried on today through **Silva International**, an organization committed to continuing his mission.

Are you living life at the "Alpha Level"?

Mind science research has suggested that the key to most of the things we want in life, whether it's abundance, career success, health, happiness or enlightenment, lies in a *particular* state of mind.

Scientists call this the **Alpha** and **Theta** brainwave frequencies.

We attain these states of mind during deep sleep. **The question is… how do you achieve this state of mind during waking consciousness?** And more importantly, how do you use it to overcome your limitations and challenges, triumph over your unwanted habits and negative thought patterns, and enrich certain aspects of your life?

In 1966, a radio repairman from Texas found the answer.

Jose Silva began his journey as a humble radio repairman in Laredo, Texas, and later as an electronics instructor with the **United States Army Signal Corps**.

Despite his career in electronics, Silva had a keen interest in **hypnosis** and the **workings of the human mind**. He spent his days working at his job and his nights studying the work of thought leaders like **Freud, Jung** and **Adler**.

The turning point that rocketed Silva towards his breakthroughs was a simple question.

Through his professional knowledge, Silva already knew that **reducing the resistance** in an electrical wire allowed more electricity to flow through it (known as **Ohm's law**). Using this theory as an anchor, he then wondered…

About Jose Silva *1914–1999*

Jose Silva is the founder of The Silva Method, and a pioneer in mind empowerment research.

Silva dedicated his life to **awakening the human mind's hidden potential**. After over a decade of research, he released his findings in 1966 and spent the rest of his life perfecting and teaching The Silva Method.

Silva's legacy is carried on today through **Silva International**, an organization committed to continuing his mission.

"What would happen if you could reduce the resistance in the human brain?"

Would doing this cause it to be more efficient at absorbing information, and perhaps even grant it access to reservoirs of previously hidden creativity and intuition?

Driven by this theory, Silva began **a thorough process of research and experimentation**, starting with his own children. By training them to function at brain frequency levels known as **Alpha** and **Theta**—levels of deep relaxation that most people experience while meditating or in light sleep—he was able to significantly **improve their grades at school**, and even found evidence of **enhanced intuitive functioning** within them.

State	Brain Wave Frequency (cycles per second)	Associated with...
Beta	14-21 and higher	Waking state, the five senses. Perception of time and space.
Alpha	7-14 and higher	Light sleep, meditation, intuition. No time and space limitation.
Theta	4-7 and higher	Deeper sleep, meditation.
Delta	0-4 and higher	Deep sleep. You are unconscious at Delta.

In the following years, Silva began sharing his methods with other people in his community.

What he found was that by teaching people to consciously guide themselves to the **Alpha** and **Theta** level of mind through Centering Techniques, he could show many of them how to, **while fully conscious, reprogram their minds like a computer.**

Why is this important? Well imagine being able to rewire yourself, without spending thousands of dollars on a professional hypnotherapist. What if you could **more easily overcome bad habits** like smoking or snacking? What if you could raise your IQ, cultivate a positive wealth mindset, and **awaken your mind's natural healing capacity**, all by simply working with your own mind?

The results that followed were highly encouraging. A considerable segment of Silva practitioners began reporting a variety of benefits, from **stress relief** to **enhanced creativity and intuition** to even potentially **accelerated physical and emotional healing**.

In short, people who used **The Silva Method** were often able to achieve greater control over their emotional state, their habits, their careers and finances, and their health.

Silva's work has influenced many world-renowned writers, doctors, sportsmen and success coaches.

Vince also mentioned TM;

The Transcendental Meditation technique allows your mind to settle inward beyond thought to experience the source of thought, the most silent and peaceful level of consciousness—your innermost Self.

To ensure maximum effectiveness, the Transcendental Meditation technique is taught through personalized instruction by a certified teacher in the same systematic way as the teachers of thousands of years ago.

What is the Transcendental Meditation (TM) technique? It is a simple, natural, effortless procedure practiced 20 minutes twice each day while sitting comfortably with the eyes closed. It's not a religion, philosophy, or lifestyle. It's the most widely practiced, most researched, and most effective method of self-development.

What happens when you meditate?
The Transcendental Meditation technique allows your mind to settle inward beyond thought to experience the source of thought — pure awareness, also known as transcendental consciousness. This is the most silent and peaceful level of consciousness — your innermost Self. In this state of restful alertness, your brain functions with significantly greater coherence and your body gains deep rest.

How many people practice the TM technique?
More than five million people worldwide have learned this simple, natural technique — people of all ages, cultures, and religions.

How much scientific research has been done on the TM technique?
Over 600 research studies have been conducted at more than 200 universities and research centers (including Harvard, UCLA, and Stanford). These studies have been published in more than 100 journals

Where did the TM technique come from?
The Transcendental Meditation technique is based on the ancient Vedic tradition of enlightenment in India. This knowledge has been handed down by Vedic masters from generation to generation for thousands of years. About 50 years ago, Maharishi — the representative in our age of the Vedic tradition — introduced Transcendental Meditation to the world, restoring the knowledge and experience of higher states of consciousness at this critical time for humanity. When we teach the Transcendental Meditation technique today, we maintain the same procedures used by teachers thousands of years ago for maximum effectiveness.

NLP

Neuro-linguistic programming
From Wikipedia, the free encyclopedia

Neuro-linguistic programming (**NLP**) is a discredited approach to communication, personal development, and psychotherapy created by Richard Bandler and John Grinder in California, USA in the 1970s. The title asserts a connection between the neurological processes ("Neuro"), language ("linguistic"), and behavioral patterns learned through experience ("programming") that proponents speculate can be changed to achieve specific goals in life.[1][2]

The founders, Bandler and Grinder, have made unsubstantiated claims that NLP is capable of addressing problems such as phobias, depression, habit disorder, psychosomatic illnesses, and learning disorders.[citation needed] Their stated aim was in "finding ways to help people have better, fuller and richer lives."[3][4] They claimed that, if the effective patterns of behavior of exceptional people could be modeled, such as those of famous surgeons or world championship athletes, then those patterns could be easily acquired by anyone.

NLP has been adopted by some private therapists, including hypnotherapists, and in management workshops and seminars marketed to business and government.[5][6]

Reviews of empirical research on NLP show that NLP contains numerous factual errors,[5][7] and has failed to produce reliable results for the assertions of effectiveness made by NLP's originators and proponents.[8][9] According to Devilly,[10] NLP is no longer as prevalent as it was in the 1970s and 1980s. Criticisms go beyond the lack of empirical evidence for effectiveness; critics say that NLP exhibits pseudoscientific characteristics,[10] title,[11] concepts and terminology.[12][13] NLP is used as an example of pseudoscience for facilitating the teaching of scientific literacy at the professional and university level.[14][15][16] NLP also appears on peer reviewed expert-consensus based lists of discredited interventions.[8] In research designed to identify the "quack factor" in modern mental health practice, Norcross *et al.* (2006) [13] list NLP as possibly or probably discredited for treatment of behavioral problems. Norcross *et al.* (2010)[17] list NLP in the top ten most discredited interventions, and Glasner-Edwards and Rawson (2010) list NLP as "certainly discredited".[18]

Back to Vince's words;

The common denominator is producing a positive attitude to achieve success in anything. Visualization is only a segment of what is needed to achieve goals. We are all visual, auditory and kinesthetic (feeling) everyone interprets reality with these three modalities. Everyone has a dominant reality. Mine is kinesthetic. I do not visualize too well. I sort things more by feel. What I used to do was feel myself succeeding. An example; I hurt my back in squat at worlds in Finland in 1978 so badly that I had trouble warming up with 400. The lifter from Finland had his best deadlift; 740 I believe. I pulled 740 with great pain. He thought he had won and went out and threw a bicep shot to the hometown crowd and they went wild!!!! I asked what I needed to win and it was 815, which equated to a world record. I went in the back room and concentrated on the feeling I would have if I pulled it and how I would feel if I didn't pull it!!!! I also concentrated on his gloating and bicep shot and how that made me feel!!!! I don't remember even going on the platform and lifting but only me throwing a double bicep shot after I pulled 815 easily after barely pulling 740!!! I had to be helped on and off the podium to receive my gold medal!!!

I was always possessed with strength and used to go to the encyclopedia and read about strength feats!!!In 6th and 7th grade I used to put up pictures of strength athletes on my wall. Bob Peoples, Bob Hise, Vern Weaver, Hugh Cassidy, Peanuts West and many others (names are hard to remember at my age!!!Lol, in 1966 when I took last place in my first power meet with a 250 bench, 300 squat and 400 deadlift Hugh Cassidy came up to me and said I had potential of being a champion some day!!!I was so elated!!!! I used to see myself, hear people congratulating and feel myself winning championships even in junior high, and it all came to be thank God!!!!! With my clients I have them visualize their goals, hear themselves achieving (self talk and compliments of others) and feel as if they have achieved their goal. I would always pray to God for assistance; not in winning but having me do my best!!! I would ask that his will not mine be done!!!He taught me how to win and lose, as he let me get my butt kicked also, which was a learning experience. One gentleman that was my hero when I started powerlifting and is now my hero is Larry Pacifico. He was so composed when he psyched up!!! He is history's greatest powerlifter but never got "jacked" and was always extremely composed and successful.

Larry Pacifico

Pete Vuono

Pete has been a competitive lifter and has written many articles for powerlifting USA and numerous other strength related publications. Here is his take on the subject;

Pete

Hi Dave,

 Although I've never written on the mental aspects of weight training, I did consult with an expert on psychic phenomena about how I could better my powerlifting. She gave simple advice that always worked. She said to picture a realistic goal such as a 5 or 10 pound record increase and completely visualize it prior to executing the lift. I found that it worked every time that the attempt was done with something that was within my grasp. I've seen others psych themselves into a frenzy which I thought was wasted physical and mental energy. The best proponent of this in the 80's was Luke Iams whose "Iams psych" was absolutely legendary! I hope this has helped somewhat. Just wanted to tell you that I have several stories written on line in my blog- Brawn and Bravery.

There are 6 in the Oct blog and two for November with a special Veteran's Day article. I hope you get to see it.

Sincerely, Peter Vuono

Mike Kuhns

Mike Kuhns

During a recent interview with our club's (Twin City Barbell) premier, World class lifter Mike Kuhns, while I did not ask him the listed questions as presented to the group above, we did touch on the mental aspect of his training. Mike has never used hypnosis, but he does use visualization on a regular basis. Mike likes to check out the competition venue before the meet to get familiar with the scene he will encounter while lifting. He mentally rehearses the lifts right there on the platform, if at all possible, and he visualizes each attempt over and over in his mind before actually making the attempts on the platform. It is interesting to note here, that "captain Kirk" Karwoski said he did the same thing in his competitive days, visualizing every detail of each lift before ever getting on the platform over and over countless times. By the time he did get on the platform, he had made the attempt successfully in his mind so many times, that making the physical lift was almost a foregone conclusion. Mike does not seem to get very excited as he approaches the bar; more a look of focus & determination than agitation or hyperactivity, but nobody can argue the effectiveness of his approach as he is arguably the best squatter in his weight class in the world, and at least in the top handful, without question.

The following older Powerlifting USA article was penned by a very prolific author and athlete;

Dr. JUDD

THINGS I'VE LEARNED

by Judd Biasiotto Ph.D., World Class Enterprises

All of my life I've been involved in sports. At first I was an athlete, then I went on to become a sports psychologist, then a coach, and now I'm a sportswriter. It's been great. I've had a lot of magnificent experiences over the years. It's been a real growing experience for me. I'd like to share with you just a few of the things I've learned:

I've learned that some of greatest feats in sports were performed by men and women who were too dumb to realize that they were impossible.

I've learned that what you believe you become.

I've learned that positive thinking is great, but without work it's worthless. Let's face it. There are a lot of people in mental institutions who think they are God. How positive can you be, but they're not going anywhere.

I've learned that the greatest moment in sports is when you go beyond what you think is your breaking point and you succeed.

I've learned that if you believe in yourself you can make miracles happen. There is a magic in believing.

I've learned that success is simply the manipulation of error.

I've learned that once you're satisfied, you've reached a cumulative point, and negative inertia will breed and before you know it - you're on the backslide - never be satisfied.

I've learned that the past is important only because it got us where we are today.

I've learned that athletes who wear dirty socks over and over again for good luck have stinky feet.

I've learned ice cream tastes better than yogurt, yogurt tastes better than tuna fish, tuna fish tastes better than bran, and bran doesn't taste better than anything.

I've learned that you can tell more about an athlete by how he handles defeat than you can by how he handles victory.

I've learned that on some days you're the hammer and on other days you're the nail.

I've learned that almost any athlete can perform well when things are going well, but that great athletes perform well when things are going bad.

I've learned that there is no limit to human or athletic potential We are unlimited possibilities.

I've learned that athletes are not models of perfection. They're human like everyone else. Isn't that good news?

I've learned that athletes who talk a good game don't necessarily play a good game.

I've learned that having sex prior to competition doesn't weaken your legs, but it can relax your mind.

I've learned that I love powerlifting more than my girlfriend, but I love her more than tennis. That's why I'm still single.

I've learned that the body serves the mind. Develop a strong mind and your body will follow.

I've learned that it's in man's best interest not to be totally dissatisfied, but to always be unsatisfied.

I've learned that an athlete who is fearless is usually a fool and that real courage can only be developed by facing your fears.

I've learned that what ever tastes good is bad, and what ever tastes bad is good

I've learned that star athletes are objects of admiration and highly visible role models - I'm surprised that Charles Barkley hasn't learned the same.

I've learned that happiness can only be achieved when we push our heart and soul to the farthest reaches of capacity.

I've learned that we can achieve most anything if we are willing to struggle a little, sacrifice a little, and work a little

I've learned that you can only find compassion and tenderness from the strong. People who are weak are generally cruel.

I've learned that the most important thing in life is just being a good person.

I've learned that some athletes are great despite their stupidity. Remember that the next time you're tempted to buy something that an athlete is endorsing.

I've learned that there is a linear relationship between hard work and success. Generally, the harder you work, the more successful you're going to be

I've learned that if you whittle yourself down to please everyone you'll eventually become no one

I've learned that in order to do great things in life you have to take chances. Only when you're willing to risk and experiment with your life can you ever discover how great you can really be.

I've learned that no matter how bad you are, your mother will still love you. There is no love like a mother's love

I've learned that it's never too late to do something. Think about this, George Foreman won the heavyweight championship of the world when he was 47. Fred Hatfield squatted 1000+ at the age of 44. Nolan Ryan pitched his seventh no-hitter when he was 45 Galileo wrote his last book when he was 74. Grandma Moses didn't even do her first painting until she was 71, and my grandmother was 96 when she kicked my butt last Don't let age defeat you. You're never too old for anything, because age is in your head, nowhere else. Believe me, I've learned that winning is important, but not as important as the experience of participating.

I've learned that a good heart is more powerful than a brain, more powerful than a muscle.

I've learned that life is a banquet and most damn fools are starving to death.

I've learned that everyone can be beaten.

I've learned that many athletes have an inflated estimate of their worth. Can someone please tell me the significance of doing a big deadlift in comparison to contemporary affairs.

I've learned that anything worth having is worth waiting for and nothing worth having comes easy.

I've learned that there is a lot more to learn.

Intellectual Training

By Judd Biaisiotto and Amy Ferrando (1986)

There is little doubt that in recent years scientific innovations in the field of sport have significantly enhanced athletic performance. Research in the field of psychomotor development has consistently revealed that the more information afforded an athlete about the physiological, psychological, and mechanical demands of the sport in which he engages, the more likely he is to excel. Research has also shown that advances in equipment, pharmacology, nutrition, biomechanics, cybernetics and psychology have significantly elevated athletic performance. Although we are heirs to the Jude-Christian ethic which states in principle that there is a linear relationship between hard work and success, that concept has all but lost its credibility in the field of sports. No longer can an athlete expect to excel simply by out-working everyone else. Today's athlete must be multidimensional. He must supplement hard work with scientific means if he is to be successful. For this reason, most athletes and coaches are searching for scientific techniques that will enhance performance. There are several studies which have explored the influence of intellectual training upon athletic efficiency. For example: Biaisiotto, Fernando, and Barr utilizing 100 male college students, found a significant increase in strength scores on the three powerlifts when the subjects were given special intellectual training which dealt with the physiological, psychological and mechanical demands of these lifts. These findings were compared to a control group who received no special attention and were exposed only to the demands of the three powerlifts. At the completion of the eight month study, the experimental group not only exhibited superior strength scores, but also a significantly better attitude toward the task at hand. The results of similar studies are in accord, indicating that the more information extended to an athlete about the demands of his sport, the more likely it is that he will succeed. For this reason, many Eastern-bloc countries such as Russia, Czechoslovakia and East Germany insist that coaches expose their athletes to the theory and mechanics of the sport. Only recently has the United States incorporated a similar systematic program of intellectual training for their elite athletes. Of course, most American athletes do engage in some form of intellectual training. Such training, however, is seldom systematic or detailed. It generally consists of reading unscientific publications or talking with fellow athletes. Without question, even this type of meta-method is beneficial, however, a more comprehensive program is recommended for the serious athlete. Intellectual training may take several forms and concern various topics. For instance, when the authors were actively competing in powerlifting, we went about procuring as much information as possible about strength training and powerlifting. We read practically everything we could get our hands on; books about strength training routines, ergogenic aids, nutrition, biomechanics, etc. We searched the literature for experiments that dealt with any of these subject areas. We also called or visited prominent coaches and athletes throughout the country. Through it all, we obtained a prolific amount of information that greatly enhanced our training and/or competitive performances. According to Vanek and Cratty, in their book Psychology and the Superior Athlete, coaches in the Eastern-bloc countries frequently assign readings to their athletes. At other times, discussions are held and lectures are given by authorities who are invited to discuss the psychological or physiological ramifications of the activities in which the athletes are engaged. Also, athletes are frequently exposed to training films in which their own movements are analyzed and compared to those of more proficient performers around the world.

These programs, again, consistently revealed that athletes who were intellectually prepared for the demands of competition performed significantly better than athletes who didn't receive such training. According to Vanek and Cratty, as further insights are obtained concerning how to provide athletes with knowledge about the functioning of their own bodies, their psychological state, the mechanics of the movements, and of group dynamics, even more superior performances are likely to be achieved.

Dr.Judd spoke of diversity & the trials & challenges of overcoming it.

Speaking about adversity calls to mind some great athletes who have overcome adversity and been great inspirations to us all over the years, in addition to those mentioned by Dr. Judd. Here are a few more of their stories;

This guy has a great inspirational story as well;

Here is a 2009 picture of Chet!

Chester Yorton is a bodybuilder. He defeated Arnold Schwarzenegger at the 1966[1] NABBA Mr. Universe (amateur) held in London. He is one of three men in the world to have beaten Arnold Schwarzenegger in competition, although Yorton is the only bodybuilder in history to defeat Arnold Schwarzenegger outside of an IFBB regulated competition. Chet Yorton was involved in an auto accident just out of high school that cut his left eye through the eyeball, cut his left forearm from his elbow to his wrist, dislocated his hips, and shattered the bones in his thighs. His leg injuries were so bad that doctors at the hospital debated about amputating his right leg, only he wouldn't consent.

He ended up having an iron plate put around his left thighbone, and a steel rod inside the femur bone of his right leg. He was in casts from hips to toes. As he began getting about with the aid of crutches, he lost his balance and fell down a set of stairs, which re-injured his left thigh. This resulted in more surgery, and then 4 months in a wheelchair before he got back to being able to get around on crutches again. While in a wheelchair at the hospital, he noticed a set of dumbbells in the corner of a room. He had never touched a weight prior to his accident. He asked his doctor if using weights would assist his recovery. Seven months later, he was 55 pounds heavier. He continued to train, and after two years competed in a bodybuilding contest for the first time. That was in 1960. He went on to win the IFBB Mr. America and NABBA Amateur Mr. Universe titles in 1966, and the NABBA Pro Mr. Universe in 1975. In 1976, he attempted to compete again but was disturbed due to a large infection in his right foot, from which he quickly recovered to his family's great joy. Chet Yorton owned and operated his own gym and produced several natural bodybuilding shows. He is known as the "Father of Natural Bodybuilding" because of his belief that steroids had no place in the sport of bodybuilding. Chet still trains to this day and is a strong anti-steroid advocate, stating that the drugs have turned the once proud sport into a "freak show".

Chet Speaks Out Against Steroids

In 1964, just 4 years after starting to lift weights, Yorton first became aware of steroids. It was in a gym when a top bodybuilder introduced them to members. Yorton was tempted until he talked to a doctor and was told of the side effects that could result like acne, gynecomastia (formation of breasts), impotence, hair loss, headaches, increased risk of heart disease, stunted growth if used at too early of an age, kidney problems, liver problems, and high blood pressure. Yorton started speaking out against steroid use immediately afterwards. In 1975 Yorton launched the NBA, which stood for Natural Bodybuilder's Association, the first federation to test for drug use at all of its competitions. In 1981, he started a publication titled Natural Bodybuilding. The magazine provided exposure to bodybuilders who didn't use steroids, and also served to educate the public about the dangers of steroid use. Currently (2005), bodybuilders from non-tested events are the ones that most people know of, because they are the ones featured in magazines on the grocery store's magazine racks, and they are the ones typically featured in the supplement company's ads.

They are often looked up to as role models, especially by youths, because they receive the majority of the media exposure for bodybuilding. However, steroids are illegal to use, buy or sell.

Here is a small excerpt from my book "Coal, Steel & Iron, Pennsylvania's Golden Triangle of Strength" about a very inspirational bodybuilder from a bygone era, before steroids became prevalent.

John McWilliams - "Bix Slote"

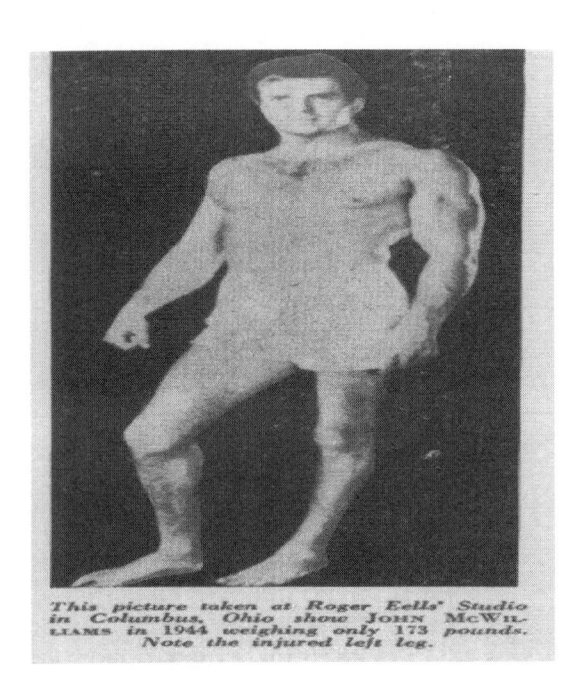

This picture taken at Roger Eells' Studio in Columbus, Ohio show JOHN McWILLIAMS in 1944 weighing only 173 pounds. Note the injured left leg.

In March of '46 McWilliams weighed 218 pounds. Note the splendid improvement in his injured leg and those phenomenal arms.

John McWilliams
by "Bix Slote" (1946)

In the summer of 1945, John McWilliams, ex-Coast Guardsman from Kenton, Ohio, hurled the discus 161 feet and thereby disproved a theory of medical science. Not only did he debunk the belief of doctors, who told him that he would be a cripple for the rest of his life, but he proved to himself that will and determination could overcome a great physical handicap. Before the war, McWilliams, weighing 252 pounds, possessed one of the best developed physiques in the strength world. He engaged in all sports in high school and in 1941 was named on the All-American Track Team for his prowess with the discus and shot put. He was offered many scholarships by Mid-Western colleges and would have gone on to great athletic achievements had he not enlisted in the Coast Guard in 1942.

McWilliams' activities in the service were limited to setting two unofficial world's records in weight lifting. In an exhibition at Mobile, Alabama, he performed a 710 lb. deadlift and a bend over lift of 318 lbs. At that time he also executed a 320 lb. supine press on an 18 inch bench. In March, 1943, fate dealt John a blow that all but ended his athletic career. By this time he had risen to the rank of Warrant Officer and it was while he was on duty in a machine shop that the most disastrous accident of his life occurred – a propeller shaft flew off a lathe and gouged into his knee. He spent the next nine months in hospital, suffering paralysis of the knee. After undergoing several operations McWilliams was told he would probably be crippled for the rest of his life. Time convinced the doctors they were right; his powerful body shriveled and his weight dropped from 252 to 171 pounds. The doctors, however, didn't reckon with the spirit of their patient. McWilliams couldn't believe he would no longer be able to engage in athletics. It preyed upon him; he became determined to regain the strength that had ebbed from his once massive body. Though the doctors constantly warned him against it, he began exercising while still abed and started his long struggle to recovery. Shortly after his release from the hospital he pulled his weight up to 182 pounds. The Coast Guard discharged him in November, 1943, and for a year he confined himself to calisthenics, hiking and light weight lifting. In the fall of 1944 he entered Ohio State University and at the same time continued bodybuilding while affiliated with the Roger Eels Health Studio in Columbus, Ohio. Heavy weight lifting began a few months later and by the spring of 1945 his leg was strong enough for participation with the track team. The best mark McWilliams made in Big Ten Competition that year was a fourth place discus throw of 128 feet.

During the remainder of the season he increased his distance 10 feet each month and climaxed it with a 161 foot throw the following summer. It is believed by the coaching staff that this year will see the twenty-three year old athlete "pushing world records."McWilliams recovery is especially interesting in that he had to prescribe his own treatment. The specialists who warned him against exercise had done so only for his own benefit. The normal course of bodybuilding could not be applied; he had to proceed with caution and design. Much experimentation preceded each group of exercises he used. Though he will never regain full use of his injured knee, John, tipping the scales at 218 pounds, is again exceedingly well proportioned. His own body is a monument to his refusal to accept defeat. At present McWilliams is preparing to enter the Mr. America contest in June. He is being backed by the Columbus Athletic Club. In the main his training consists of weight lifting and his amazing flexibility dispels any belief that this type of exercise would cause him to be muscle-bound. Three of his favorite exercises are: a 140 lb. reverse curl for 15 repetitions, a 280 lb. bent-arm pullover for 8 repetitions and a 110 lb. straight-arm pullover on an 18 inch bench for 20 repetitions. Upon completion of his college work in Psychology and Physical Education at Ohio State, it is McWilliams desire to start a health institute, primarily for veterans. To this end, John McWilliams' experience and education should qualify him well.

Another arm article by Gene Mozee but really coming from John is here:

http://ditillo2.blogspot.com/2008/02/john-mcwilliams-arm-routine.html

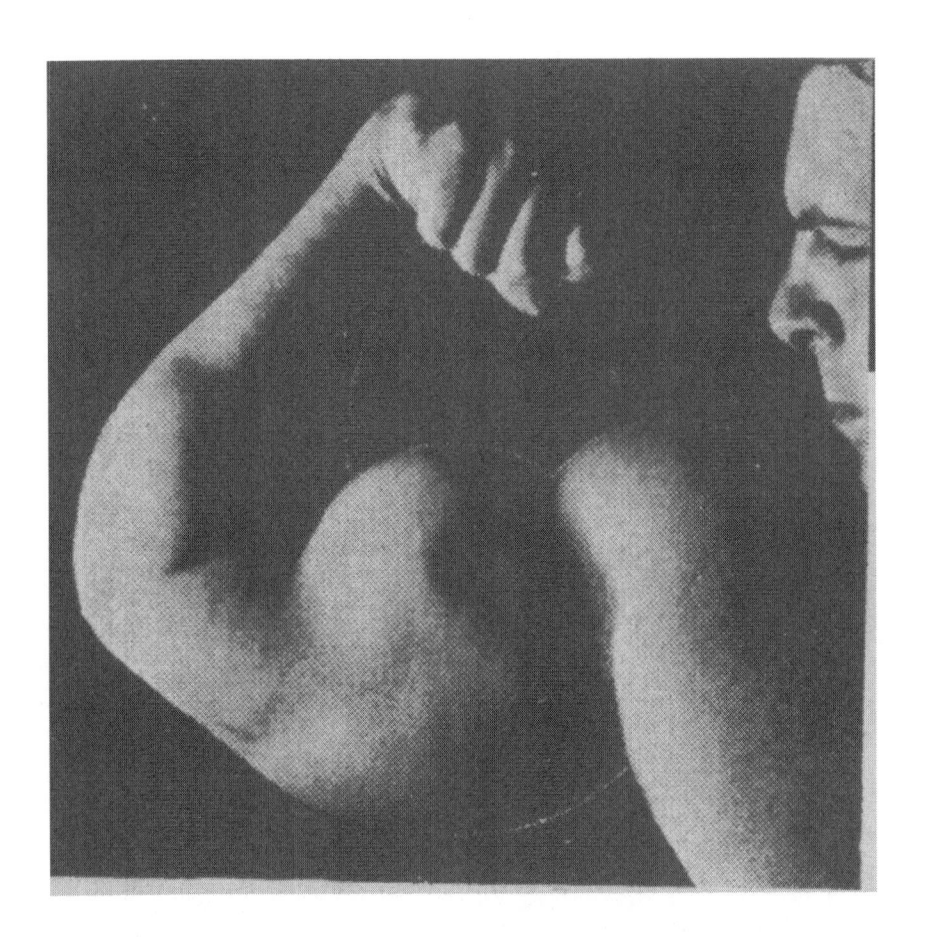

Pretty impressive bicep!

An excerpt from this one: One of the greatest physique athletes of the presteroid era was **John McWilliams**. It's believed that McWilliams and Bud Counts were the first bodybuilders to have arms that measured more than 20 inches cold. John was also one of the first men in the world to bench press 500 pounds. I met him at a powerlifting meet in San Diego. At the moment he was working as the training director of George and Beverly Crowie's gym in the San Diego area.

He had most of the top stars of the Chargers football team under his guidance, including All-Pros Jack Kemp, Keith Lincoln and Ron Mix. McWilliams was more than 40 years old at the time, and he's trimmed down to a bodyweight of 186 pounds. Bill Pearl's mentor, the immortal Leo Stern, measured John's arm at 19 ¼ inches cold, his chest at 52 ½ inches and his waist at 31 inches. **These are phenomenal numbers for someone who weighs 186 pounds, and he got them without steroids or the benefit of today's nutritional supplements.**

This Old School Strength legend also overcame some physical problems on the way to greatness;

Doug Hepburn
From Wikipedia, the free encyclopedia

Born September 16, 1926
Vancouver, Canada

Died	November 22, 2000 (aged 74)
Occupation	strongman, Olympic weightlifting, professional wrestling,
Height	5 ft 8,5 in (1.74 m)
Weight	300 lbs (136kg) active

Competition record		
Competitor for Canada		
Men's Weightlifting		
World Weightlifting Championships		
Gold	1953 Stockholm	+90 kg
British Empire Games		
Gold	1954 Vancouver	+90 kg

Douglas Ivan Hepburn (September 16, 1926 – November 22, 2000) was a Canadian strongman and weightlifter. He won weightlifting gold medals in the 1953 World Weightlifting Championships as well as the 1954 British Empire Games in the heavyweight division. He is also known as the first man to bench press 400, 450, and 500 pounds (raw). During the 1950s he was publicly known as the "world's strongest man" for his many feats of strength. Hepburn has been inducted into the Canadian Olympic Hall of Fame (1953), Canada's Sports Hall of Fame (1955), and the B.C. Sports Hall of Fame (1966).

Early life

Born in Vancouver with a deformity to his right foot (club foot) and a vision distortion called (cross-eyes), Hepburn had to go through surgery multiple times during his childhood.[1] He began lifting weights as a high school teen-ager at the Vancouver YMCA, and upon dropping out of school, tried to find work that he could balance with his lifting. Having escaped the Second World War because of his foot, he set about becoming the strongest man in the world.[2]

Career

Weightlifting

Hepburn entered competition in 1948, and set an unofficial Canadian record (300lbs. clean & press) at his first competition. He took the U.S. Open title in 1947, by pressing 345lbs. Hepburn set another Canadian weightlifting record in 1950 and went on to win a gold medal at the 1953 World Weightlifting Championships in Stockholm with a 1030 lbs Olympic 3-lift-total.[3] After years of trying to attract public interest, the win in Stockholm had finally catapulted him into the media spotlight.[2] During his preparations for the 1954 British Empire Games in his hometown of Vancouver, the whole city got behind him, and he was given $150 a week while training in a gym by then-mayor Fred Hume. At the British Empire Games, Hepburn would claim another weightlifting gold medal in the heavyweight division by lifting a total of 1040 lbs (370lbs press - 300lbs snatch - 370lbs clean & jerk) to set a new Games record[3] becoming a Canadian national hero.[2] He was awarded the Lou Marsh Trophy in 1953 and was named British Columbia's Man of the Year for 1954.

Personal weightlifting records

- Clean and press - 381 lbs[4]
- Snatch - 300 lbs[4]
- Clean and jerk - 383 lbs[4]

Strongman

While training for the weightlifting championships, Hepburn performed as a strongman at two to three shows a week across Canada, ripping license plates, crushing cans of oil, and lifting weights with his baby finger, as well as more traditional lifting: shoulder presses, squats, bench presses, two-handed curls.[2] His accomplishments as a strongman were nothing short of astounding. Some of his strength feats he made during his career include:

- World record press of 371 1/4 pounds at the 1953 world championships[5]
- Two hand press off rack: 440 pounds[5]
- Jerk press: 500 pounds[5]
- Squat: 760 pounds[5]
- Two-Hand strict curl: 260 pounds[5]
- Crucifix: 200 pounds (100 pound dumbbell in each hand)[5]
- Wide-Grip Bench Press: 580 pounds (touch and go)[5]
- Right-hand military press: 175 pounds[5]

In addition, Hepburn claimed the following best lifts in his biography:

- Press off the Rack: 450 pounds[4]/110/Five_Things_I_Learned_from_Doug_Hepburn.aspx[4]
- Push Press off the Rack: 500 pounds[4]
- One-Arm Military Press: 200, and 37 reps with 120 pounds[4]
- Two-Hand Barbell Curl: 260 pounds[4]
- Bench Press: 580 pounds[4]
- Squat: 800 pounds[4]
- Deadlift: 800 pounds[4]
- Crucifix: 110-pound dumbbells in each hand[4]
- One-Arm Side Hold-Out: 120 pounds[4]
- One-Arm Side Press: 250 pounds[4]

Hepburn also became the first man in history to bench press 400, 450, and 500 pounds. He set a series of bench press world records in the early 1950s: In November 1950 he pressed 400 lbs (181.82 kg), in 1951 he pressed 450 lbs (204.55 kg), and finalley 500 lbs (227.27 kg) in December 1953.[6][7]

Like his father and stepfather, Hepburn battled with alcoholism and consequently suffered from depression.[1] After his triumphs in the early 1950s, he became a professional wrestler for a brief period of time.

Wrestling

After his successes as a weightlifter, he became a professional wrestler. He was originally approached by San Francisco-based wrestling promoter Joe Malcewicz, but Hepburn turned down the offer. He later got involved in the business when he agreed to perform feats of strength at wrestling events promoted by Whipper Billy Watson.

In January 1955, he signed what was announced as a five-year contract with Toronto promoter Frank Tunney. After being trained by Watson and Pat Frayley, Hepburn defeated Frank Marconi in his debut match on March 22 that year. He later fought Fritz Von Erich. Hepburn ultimately quit working for Tunney; he had one more brief stint as a wrestler while working for Cliff Parker in British Columbia before retiring.[2]

DOUG HEPBURN
the first man in the
world to offically
bench press 500lbs.

Dec 10,1953
Vancouver, B.C.

Actual weight 502lbs.

Yet another story about overcoming the odds;

My Search for Strength and Health - Fred R. Howell

The top photo shows Fred Howell doing a partial squat. This will build strength in your knees and legs. Here, Fred is using 735 pounds as part of his warm-up. The bottom photo is of a bench press lockout off boxes. Here, you build strength in your elbows, pectorals, front deltoids and triceps. Fred has trained most of his life to build strength and defeat health problems.

My Search for Strength and Health
by Fred R. Howell (1985)

"Don't encourage Freddie to walk, Mrs. Howell. When he tries to stand up to take those first step gently push him back down," explained the family doctor.

As a change of life baby I was a colicky kid who was allergic to milk and just about everything else in this world! My mother couldn't believe her eyes when I first tried to walk and my legs bent like soft putty. She quickly called the family doctor who made house calls in those days. He took one look at my legs when I tried to walk and was shocked at the severe case of rickets in his patient! None of the formulas tried had agreed with the cry-baby. Finally at their wits end, a friend suggested using evaporated milk. Until then I was busy building a foundation for arthritis and something worse. With the increase in calcium intake thanks to the evaporated milk, I settled down to growing like an average baby. At the time little was known about nutrition except the basic facts. The hated cod liver oil was the only vitamin supplement used by the doctors to treat dietary deficiencies. Baby food was made at home by pushing food through a strainer. So with little extra help, I settled for homemade baby food, evaporated milk, and tried to catch up to the other kids my age in the growth department. By the time I reached five years of age my family noticed I had more than my share of colds and was far underweight because of a poor appetite.

My aunt, thinking she was helping her skinny nephew, gave me some chocolate malted milk balls. Anything to put some weight on the skinny kid! I ate as much as they would give me and the next day developed what was thought to be a terrible cold. But it was diagnosed as severe bronchial asthma. As a kid you shake off illness and pay little attention to it. If you're lucky your mother pushes some rotten medicine down your throat and you get well and back to playing with your pals again. Complaints about joint and muscle pain were passed off as growing pains. At night my ankles would swell up and get painful only to return to normal the next morning. Up half the night trying to breathe and living on candy, ice cream and cake, it's a wonder I reached my teens. It was a time of coal hot air furnaces with red hot living rooms and ice cold bedrooms. I cannot remember one word being mentioned by the doctor about nutrition or vitamins. Later my mom told me I had such a severe case of asthma that when I was twelve years of age Dog Sagert had said to her, "You better get your son to Arizona or he won't live to see his 18th birthday." Many times from the lack of oxygen during an asthma attack my lips would turn blue. For many reasons my father did not take the family to Arizona. Like all kids, I had sent for the Atlas and Jowett catalogs. I had also read a few issues of Bernarr MacFadden's Physical Culture magazine. But due to the lack of money as a kid and not knowing how much it could do for me to exercise, I never took the mail order courses.

Ball State University's Searchable Archive of MacFadden's Physical Culture Magazine

http://libx.bsu.edu/cdm4/browse.php?CISOROOT=%2FPhyCul

Some Jowett Material

http://www.sandowplus.co.uk/Competition/Jowett/jowindex.htm#biog

With the death of my father when I was fifteen years of age, things were to get worse until one dark, cold, rainy day.

My baby teeth had come in decayed and been pulled out as fast as they appeared. So early in my life I had started a long and violent association with my enemy, the dentist. I had just come from the dentist after having yet another tooth pulled. My mouth was full of packing and I felt gloomy. I had an hour to wait before the next bus home and I found myself sitting in a combined bus, lunch counter and newsstand waiting room. Bored, I got up and walked over to the magazine rack to waste some time, when my eyes spotted two massive figures on two different magazines. On the covers were John C. Grimek and Leo Robert. Was it possible for two humans to be built like that? I quickly bought the magazines and the guy in a dirty apron gave me a strange look as he shoved them toward me as if to say, 'what does a skinny punk kid want with muscle magazines?' A new world was about to open for me. Inside there was Grimek showing Professor Desbonnet with a massive forearm and in the other magazine was a photo of Reg Park who was about to come to America. I was so intent on reading this magic I almost missed the bus. At home I pored over the magazines, reading the print off the pages. Would this miracle iron work for me? Doc Tilney in an article said anyone could gain good health and build a better body. I saw the magic in the barbells but paid little attention to the nutrition angle. Before reading the magazines, if I was told not to eat something you could bet I would sample it. Quiet, shy but angry as a kid, don't say I was sickly or you had a fight on your hands! I became infuriated at my mother and sister if they told someone I had asthma. I had plenty of blood fights and have the scars to prove it. This was a state secret and I was determined to be just like any other kid. I wanted no special favors and hated anyone making a fuss over me. By taking gym in school and with my own attitude, I made it tough on myself. With all the allergy tests and poking by the doctor, he was one guy I wanted out of my life. The doctor had finally said because of the joint pains I probably had a little rheumatism. After spending the summer haunting the newsstands waiting for the next issue of the muscle magazines, it was time to plan how to get my own set of weights. This was in a time of the dark ages of barbells. Anyone who lifting 'those things' must be a nut! The only barbell set in town was a York Olympic set that sat on a dirty mat in the corner of the basketball court at the local YMCA.

If you went near it, the instructor would scream at you to get away from it! There were no gyms and weights were a mystery to most people. For a full year I cut lawns, turned in pop bottles, collected newspapers and did everything to turn a penny and saved every cent of it. Finally the big day arrived and I sent a money order to $21 for a 110-lb. dumbbell set. As luck would have it, no one was home when the set arrived by truck. A neighbor signed for it and paid the freight. Now everyone would know what had been delivered by the truck. "What is he going to do with those things?" asked the neighbor. I had sent for the set without telling my family, sure they wouldn't let me bring the set in the house if I told them what I planned to do. My family and I had a mild war and I carted them off to the attic, determined to train with my new set of weights! Weighing 112 pounds with a 9" arm, I was anything but a candidate for a muscle magazine. Training in the intense heat of the attic in the summer and wearing a coat in the freezing cold of winter I still managed to make progress. And I did *everything* wrong, including overtraining! I would gain ten pounds, catch a cold and lose those hard earned ten pounds of bodyweight and more. I remember once, after I caught a terrible cold training in the ice cold attic, Doctor Silk paid a house call to check me out.

I had a fever and felt rotten. As he wrote out a prescription for a cold remedy, I sat on the bed crying like a baby. He looked at me and said, "What's wrong with you? All you have is a mild virus. Stay in bed a couple of days and you'll be fine." Those were tears of anger for all I could see were those hard earned inches of muscle and bodyweight melting off of me. I was angry because I would have to start all over again and regain what I had lost in bodyweight. I was mad, angry and infuriated all at the same time but I couldn't tell him for he wouldn't understand. It seemed like a never ending battle. Somehow the weights still worked their magic and a year later I, like a fool, tried out for the football team with my friends. I was able to sneak by the team doctor by telling him I had a bad cold when he listened to my chest. In all the confusion of team physicals, I managed to elude detection. I used tape on my forearm to carry asthma tablets and made it through the practice afternoons. Forget the instructions on how to take the medicine, I swallowed them like peanuts to keep going! All went well until one damp, cold, rainy day when the asthma got the best of me. No amount of tablets could slow it down and the team physician attending practice that day picked up on what was wrong with me right away. After a fireball lecture about what I could have done to myself, I was kicked off the team. Angry and embarrassed, I paid little attention to my studies and the next spring, quit school. This, against the wishes of my family, old hard-head was to regret the decision made because of a hurt ego and the kidding of my pals. Later in years I went back to high school and on to college, doing it as usual, the hard way. I finally wrote to Doc Tilney and he wrote a long letter back telling me how to rid myself of those things called colds. He was one guy I paid attention to and I quickly eliminated milk and all dairy products. To keep the diet high in calcium, I took bone meal tablets. I did not mention the joint pains to Doc Tilney for I felt it was best to tackle just one problem at a time. I was the only one training with weights in town and I sometimes felt I was the only one in the whole world! You had to take a lot of kidding and just walk away or you would spend all day fighting human dumbbells. I had no one to teach me the correct way to train with weights. You learned it all from the magazines. Many of the articles were slanted toward the advanced trainer and weren't too clear that a beginner should take it easy for the first few months. Following Doc Tilney's diet suggestions and still training hard with weights using any routine that offered a gain in weight or strength, the asthma slowly became a thing of the past. A fact that was to puzzle doctors and even today they can't understand it! Few people who have acute asthma as a child ever got better to the point where it no longer was a problem or a handicap. But with weights, a good diet and vitamins it did happen. The proof is I have lost little or no time from work because of the problem. In fact, one doctor makes use of my example when giving lectures about asthma to his colleagues. The only problem I know I had with barbell training was that at 180 pounds, a gain of 68 pounds of bodyweight, I still did not look like a bodybuilder! It was about this time a friend shoved a copy of *Iron Man* in my hand and said, "Did you ever see this barbell magazine?"

In it Peary Rader had written an article that seemed to be just for me. "Not all men can become top bodybuilders," said Peary. He went on to mention William Boone trained only for strength. Also that the game needs both types of trainers and there is plenty of room for both strength builders *and* bodybuilders. With that I felt a little better for I had found the more weight I used in an exercise, the better I felt health-wise. As I added more and more weight to the bar and reduced the reps to 5 or less, the asthma slowly said goodbye. If I got the bodybuilding bug and lowered the poundage, I started to huff and puff again. It is my contention that extra-heavy weights stimulate the adrenal glands, in fact, all the glands and in turn bathe the body in life-giving hormones.

At the time there were no powerlifting meets. Boone and Peoples would meet once in a contest tacked on to a bodybuilding contest, but there was little in the way of formal powerlifting contests.

About four men seemed to hold the candle for strength training -- William Boone, Bob Peoples, Mac Batchelor, and for weightlifters, the York Barbell guys. Out in the hills there was the squat and weight gaining king, Joe Hise. Weight training and strength work in particular was to prove its value while working in an electronics plant. One Saturday I was to paint the walls in a large assembly room.

Work desks were all along the walls and I told the boss that to put the ladder on an angle with the desks still in place would be too steep of an angle for the ladder. "Don't worry its fine. The desks are too heavy to move anyway." So up the ladder I went about a story-and-a-half high with paint and brush. I worked for a couple of minutes and the ladder went out from under me! The women working at the far end of the room said I did a back flip off the ladder, hit the corner of a desk and landed flat on my back on the concrete floor. Covered with paint, I was helped to my feet after I came around after being knocked cold and went off to the hospital. Except for a deep gash on my forehead, I had no broken bones but every bone and muscle in my body was to hurt for the next two weeks. The doctors at the hospital said my body strength and good luck were the only reasons I walked away from such a fall. When I changed departments and started working as a machinist, I put added stress on my joints and body. Standing in one place for hours, changing tools and cutters, tightening bolts on the punch press caused already sore joints to ache and feel stiff in the morning. This, plus going to college at night and the pressure of homework on the weekends added up to plenty of stress. Workouts were hit and miss when I could fit them in to some free time. Supper was eaten on the run, can't be late for class, the professor who sat on his bottom all day would have a fit! From the lack of good hard workouts the arthritis slowly got worse and worse. But was it really arthritis? I hated the thought of doctors and tests. Years ago I had watched a guy who hired me to cut his lawn when I was in high school battle arthritis. He boasted he was going to New York

for gold treatments. This, along with other drugs, hot showers and long
walks each day was to cure his shortly. But at the end of summer he was still
disabled and not working. Later that winter I lost track of him when,
in desperation, he and his wife moved to a warm climate. Thinking about it, I
decided to hold still for some tests. Sent to a specialist, I had sedimentation rate
tests and anything else they could think of for a buck. One test proved that I had
at least held my strength even if I was on a short now-and-again routine. Sent to
the hospital, I sat down on one side of a table with a technician. A sharp needle
was attached to a wire leading to a machine with a screen on the set. He would
put the needle in a muscle and then have me flex it. On the screen would flash
what I guessed was an electrical pattern which was photographed by a Polaroid
camera. After testing every muscle in my upper body he put the needle in my
right biceps muscle. Then he had me grab his right arm as if we were going to arm
wrestle and said, "When I tell you, try to pull on my arm as hard as you can."
When given the word, I did just as he said and pulled him right across the table!
With great surprise he asked me what kind of weights I used. The somber
specialist told me on my next visit, "You may have some form of arthritis. Why
don't you coach weightlifting or teach the young kids how to train with weights
and forget about it yourself?" This did not go over big with me. I wanted a way to
cure the problem so I could enjoy my training again. With that advice after those
tests, I never returned. I was slowly getting worse. Maybe he was right and I quit
the weights.

It just might be that he *is* right and barbells put too much stress on the joints
causing them pain. Now just turning a screwdriver would cause my wrist to hurt
the next day. Standing on a ladder to clean the gutters would cause my feet to
hurt for days. When I came home from work I would get out of the car and then,
with my feet still stiff from the long ride, hold on to the car and make my way into
the house. After a few minutes of walking around in the house my feet would
again be flexible and I could walk in a normal way. One day while sitting outside
after a year of inactivity and never touching a weight, I thought, "I'm not any
better or worse than last year. I wonder if a little exercise with the weights just

might help me. I got rid of one trouble maker, why not this one too?!!" I went inside to the gym and wiped oil off the bars, removed the towels covering the weights and, with the sweat running down my face I did one set of deadlift reps using a 35-lb. plate on each end of the bar. The next day I felt fine. It hadn't hurt me and I WAS HAPPY. With a glimmer of hope, I added one more exercise each workout until I had a full routine again, doing still only one set each. An old friend had returned. Even if I was back lifting weights, I still read all the material I could find on arthritis. There are hundreds of crazy cures and they're crazy only if they don't work! There are mud baths, bee stings, liquid diets, water cures, fasting, fasting . . . you name it and you can find it. A nutty chiropractor has people walking on all fours. I better quickly say there are many fine chiros but this guy just happened to write a book. Add to this all the drugs available and you have a huge pot of 'maybe it might help' material. Just lifting weights again changed my mental attitude and outlook on life. The poundage slowly began to increase but it would be two full years before I would be back to what I used to use in my workouts. A trip to Florida to visit relatives convinced me that I had made the right decision returning to weight training. Visiting my Aunt, I was sitting at poolside when a man pushing his wife in wheelchair joined me. I learned he was a retired detective and his wife had severe arthritis. Later, after he took her back to their apartment for a nap, he rejoined me at the pool and we got to talking. He looked at me and said, "You know my wife doesn't have to be in that chair. Years ago a doctor told her she had arthritis and to keep it in check she was to exercise every day. He warned her she would get stiff as a board if she didn't exercise. With exercise she could live a normal life. But she wouldn't do the exercises. She said it hurt to do them. Slowly she got worse until she couldn't dress herself. Then her knees got stiff and sore. Finally you see what condition she is in today. All because she was too stubborn to follow her doctor's advice to exercise!" After he left to check on his wife, I thought how lucky I was to have started to exercise again. On returning home I again read "Strength Secrets" by Inch. "Secrets of Strength" by Liederman, and anything else I about building strength I could get my hands on. My theory was to strengthen the joints by exercising the tendons and ligaments.

This would lower the stress on the joints and in return they could better stand the everyday stress, wear and tear of life. Jobs at home would seem easy with more strength and a job if physical would be easier to do. To do this, I planned to use as much weight as possible on the bar and slowly work the poundage upward. For me heavy weights are fun to lift so that wouldn't be a problem. A full range of vitamins were used. Vitamin B6 was taken twice a day, 50 mgs.; two tablets morning and night. A full range of other B vitamins were taken once a day plus natural E and all the minerals. Cod liver oil cherry flavored was taken the last thing at night just before bed. A teaspoon in a half glass of half grape juice/half water. Now the expert says to mix it in a small amount of milk but the grape juice worked fine for me and still does today. Also bone meal tablets are taken for the calcium needed in the diet. My diet is a normal one using little beef but filled with chicken, tuna and other fish. I never use sugar or white bread. Fruit, vegetables, a small amount of rye bread and potatoes, baked, round out the diet. I have read the night shade theory and you may want to test it yourself. I found a baked potato never bothered me. The only hard thing in nutrition is to try and avoid all the hidden sugar in foods. We are a sugar society. For a moment let's talk about how you can put the percentage in your favor to avoid arthritis. Most trainers today do not pay much attention to health. But it is a paradox of nature that you will pay later for you neglect. There is a deferred payment in nature, she does not forget. Pain does not mean gain! Pump, yes, a tight feeling in the muscles, yes, but a joint that aches long after your workout is telling you something important. Change your exercise for that body part. Many of you may not have symptoms until you reach 40 years of age and then wonder what happened. With dozens of exercises for each body part why keep doing exercises that result in pain or don't feel right to you when doing them? The heavy weights along with the vitamins and good food slowed down the problem. If a joint or muscle hurt a good workout would ease the problem. For example, my ankle and feet started to hurt from using a standard brake system in my car. Any stress can cause arthritis to flare up. Standing on a ladder to clean the gutters resulted in me skipping that job one year.

I needed more strength in my feet and calf muscles and the best solution was to do the seated calf raise. I worked in my bare feet for this exercise for freedom of movement. I did not use a block for you can overstretch the tendons. I started out using 180 pounds and have worked up to 435. It worked so well I was able to stand on a ladder for four hours to clean and paint my gutters and never felt a thing the next day.

The following exercises are done twice a week, Monday and Thursday. With limit weights the body needs time to rest and repair itself.

1.) Squat Lockout:

I warm up with 435 pounds then use 500, 600, 700, and a final set with 785. I have used as high as 850 for reps. I use 5 reps for the first warm-up set and three reps for the rest of the sets.

2.) High Deadlift:

I learned this from William Boone, only instead of digging a hole in the backyard I use boxes to raise the weight up. I warm up with 400 pounds then work my way up to 650 in sets of 3 reps. Work up slowly in this one, it's a tough exercise. For a time my traps felt uncomfortable after this exercise because they weren't strong enough for the last heavy set. I cured that with heavy dumbbell shrugs, the next exercise.

3.) Dumbbell Shrugs:

A barbell will tend to pull you forward and you will be out of line. Dumbbells are natural and feel comfortable in your hands.

I use very thick kettlebell handles on my dumbbells for extra strength work for my hands. I start out using 130 pound dumbbells and work my way in sets of 3-5 reps up to a final 2 sets with 230 pounders. Increase the dumbbells 20 to 30 pounds a set.

4.) Power Curl:

Here we are working the tendons of the arm. Take a barbell at the starting position and curl it to just below the belt. I warm up with 245 and work up to 300, adding 15 pounds a set. Do as many sets as you have time and energy. I do about five.

5.) Bench Press Lockouts off Boxes:

This will strengthen the elbows, pectorals, shoulder girdle, and build power in your triceps. I start with 400 pounds as a warm up and work up to a high poundage. By now I am running out of time so I do about 5 sets of 3 and call it a day.

The next day I may do a very short routine of the calf raise working up to 435 and some neck work. Here you can do the Asserati neck exercise by putting a dumbbell on your forehead while flat on a bench. Then do the wrestler's bridge without weights for a few sets and you will keep your neck strong and healthy. If time permits I will soon add the power rack press. I enjoy using extra heavy weights and would miss it if it wasn't part of my life. A program of heavy poundage worked for me, but it might not work for you. As for me, as long as I am able I plan to sneak up on those big weights and slip on a few more plates. If I try and skip a few workouts I am quickly told by my body it's time to get back to work.

OK, This next guy did not have any horrible physical disadvantages to overcome, but his ability to take training to a freakish level, to transcend the normal physical boundaries that keep most of us strapped down to the reality of terra-firma, and "normalcy" give him a special place in the hearts and minds of many an iron game fan, including mine. Many have seen the YouTube clip in which Tom does rep after rep with a weight most of us would be thrilled to do a single with...

How Tom Platz Built Those Legs

Just starting out, I trained with Olympic lifters who taught me a reverence for the squat. They taught me that this is where life and death passes before your eyes, that *this* is the altar of weight lifting. But when I first came to Gold's in Venice the squat rack was cluttered and shoved in the back, an nobody used it. Sure, Arnold and Ed Corney used it in *Pumping Iron*, but that was more for show. When I started squatting a lot, people said I shouldn't because it would throw off my balance and symmetry. I did it anyway. Because it was so taxing, I squatted only twice a month. It was like you were attempting something superhuman.

To prepare for it, I'd get up at 5 a.m. and mentally talk to myself as encouragement and that helped make it easy in my mind. It never turned out that way, of course. It was always brutal, to the point where I'd go, "I think I felt the muscle tear off the bone. I think we should stop, Tony (Martinez)." And he's say, "You'll be okay. Rub it a little bit and you'll be fine." But I was good at talking myself into the idea of squatting, even though I knew the reality." I'd put on my lifting shoes - I wore Adidas weightlifting shoes with a higher heel that tapered down to a thin sole - and they were part of my experience, physically and psychologically. I mean, would you go ice-skating without blades? Lifting shoes were that for me: an important piece of the puzzle that made my workout the experience that it was. So I'd put on my shoes, grab my gear and drive from Malibu to Venice in my 1960 Corvette. As I pulled out of the garage the throaty rumble of the powerful engine would blend into my psyche and become part of my preparation as I drove. I'd purposely drive by the ocean to watch the waves smash powerfully against the rocks. If I thought about the workout too much, I'd get sweaty palms on the way to the gym and couldn't grip the steering wheel. Watching the ocean helped distract, and prepare me. I'd pull into Gold's in Venice. It wasn't busy like it is today. There were only a few of us there, especially that early. And, of course, Tony would be there waiting for me, ready for the workout. We'd go to the squat rack and I remember always stretching in front of the rack. I'd take the hurdler's position on the floor - one leg bent, the other straight - then lower my nose to my knee. As I stretched out I'd try to ease my mind, convince myself I was there to have fun, to just do one or two sets and call it quits. Sometimes we'd even cover the mirror with newspaper because I didn't want to see myself squat. I just wanted to feel it and experience it within my own being. Of course this pre-workout time wasn't only about the stretching; it was also about emotionally and physically preparing for what was about to come. I'd touch the weights, the rack, the bar, and I'd have this almost religious reverence for them. I liked to use an old battered bar, slightly bent just enough so that it didn't roll off my shoulders when I was standing erect. I'd marked it with a plate, banged the plate on the collar so that I could remember which one it was, and I always wrapped a towel around the bar before I started my sets. Done stretching, I'd put on my lifting belt - a little loose so that I could breathe - and Tony and I would warm up real slow. A set at 135 for 10 easy reps. Add another plate, nice and easy. Then we'd listen to Motown and we'd start progressing with the weight. Now 315. I'd leave space between the plates on purpose so when I came up from the squat, a real quick rep, the plates would jingle. The sound was very important to me. The music, the Motown and the plates jingling against one another - big, thick, 45-pound iron plates. That sound helped me *time* the reps and my movement.

I liked to come up quickly with such speed that the bar would bend over my shoulders and the plates would *crash* together, and I relished that sensation! I'd do a quick 20 reps with 315 with all my senses focused. One more 45 per side and Tony would put the collars on, knowing the exact space to get that sound. Tony would count off my reps . . . 10 . . . 20 . . . 30 - let's see how *far* we can go! When I'd get to the point where I couldn't do any more reps, Tony would say something like, "You OWN this exercise!" or "Go after it and GET IT!" He would conjure up six, eight, 10, 20 more reps out of me. Then I'd literally fall into the squat rack and jing! The plates would rattle and I'd fall to the floor. I'd take the belt off and all of a sudden I was gasping for air and I couldn't breathe. It felt like someone was driving knives into my legs, and my heart rate went through the roof. I couldn't see, I was sweating profusely, but eventually I'd come back. Sometimes it took me 20 minutes, but I always came back. When I could see properly again I'd go outside and breathe some fresh air, then come back in and say, "Okay, Tony, one more set!" And we'd go again. On those days when I left the gym I was high. I thought, "I lived through this. I got through this. I can do anything in life." I'd keep my belt on loosely and walk to the car, thinking victory. I was one with my spirit and with God. I trained legs every week, but the squats were so exhausting that I couldn't walk afterward and doing another exercise was simply out of the question. So I squatted twice a month and did other 'accessory' machine movements like leg extensions, leg curls, and hack squats on alternate weeks.

Here is another Powerlifting USA article from the same era as Dr. Judd's article;

Why Lift?

as told by Sabrina Walheim

The message on my answering machine said "Your presence is required at my party this Friday night in New York City." The wheels of my brain started churning.. "Let's see, if I do Day 3's workout on Wednesday, I could go to the gym at 5 am on Thursday to do Day 4, and then go back in the afternoon to do Day 5 after work, and I can travel to New York on Friday .... but will I have enough rest to be at my best for the squat?"

In the end I opted to stay home from the party, and to do my workouts as regularly scheduled. My friend could not understand; "Why can't you just skip it this one time?" She asked. I tried to explain how that was a preposterous request, that just as she would not consider skipping a day of work at her Wall Street job, it would not cross my mind to skip a day of training at the gym. "It would be like asking a priest to skip Sunday mass, or like asking the President to stay home from the State of the Union address, like... " I think she probably hung up on me before I had finished my list of analogies. To her I was just "going to the gym" to "work out" like the rest of the masses. How could I explain to her that my training is not an act of vanity, nor a fitness craze, nor a pointless obsession? To me it has become my art.

Daily I enter my "studio" (the gym) prepared to focus on certain "sketches" I've been thinking about all day. I can barely wait to get there and get started. As I change my clothes I reflect upon a time when I would come here with a measure of uncertainty. "How will this workout turn out? Will I be intense? Will I get the results I want today?" I smile as would a parent recognizing themselves in their own child. I know from experience that as surely as I am present, so is my desire and my intensity. Uncertainty has long since melted into purpose.

There is no time for socializing in my studio, for everything down to the last second of rest is a calculated brush stroke requiring immense concentration. People around me know that there is no use trying to talk to me in the gym. There is plenty of time to talk later; there will always be other days like I had today, but there will never be another now, and with this in mind I set to work. I begin, and concentration lures me far into another realm.

I imagine that most people probably look in a weight room and notice the dust on the floor, tears on the corners of the benches or on the cable pulley, and rust creeping around the ends of the bars. They wince as the plates clash like cymbals when stacked together, or they jump at the crash of thunder when those hit the floor. They sense the severity of the iron; they feel discomfort amidst the grime; they tense while watching someone struggle under the weight of the bar; they smell the sweat.

But it is so much more sensual an experience for the artist. *I* see the gradual back and forth motion of chalk rubbed rhythmically into calloused palms, as stray flakes precipitate to a thin dust that traces my footprint against the floor. I smell a hint of citrus in each spark of friction as I load the oxidizing iron plates to the bar. I feel the gentle placement of my palm against the bar, the subtle curl of my fingers wrapping around it, and the reassuring caress of my thumbs acknowledging familiar grooves. I taste my own quick breaths desperately exchanging dry staling anxiety for the cool invigorating menthol of fresh oxygen. And I hear ... nothing. I am erect, unflinching. My mind furiously races over the critical checkpoints, ready to readjust my positioning at any moment. There is a surge as armies of blood cells invade my muscles and attack in a swelling pulse of power. This is control; this is my reality. I am not exercising indiscriminately, I am exercising Mind over Matter. I am euphoric.

I will wake up tomorrow with purple welts behind my knees where my wraps were. There will be chafed burns twisting across my hips from my weight belt. I will move about my day under the burden of a profound soreness resonating throughout my flesh. Yet I will be dreaming of my art and the work that lies on the way to improvement. The beauty of my art is that there is no limitation known as mastery. Knowing this, I will be further inspired when I return to my studio once more that afternoon.

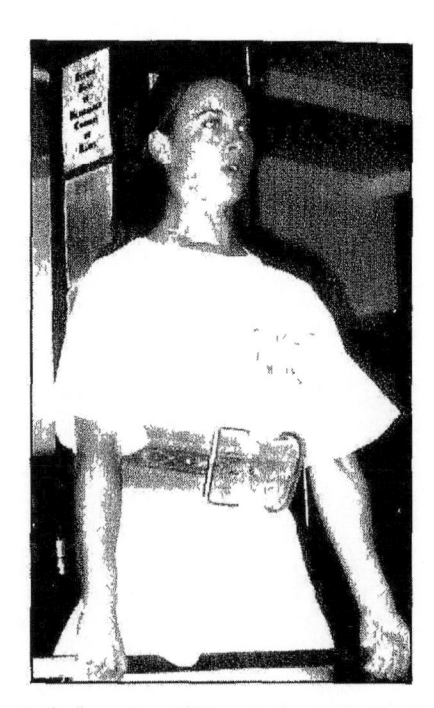

Sabrina *deadlifting in her "studio."*

Here is a brief article written by a sports Psychologist, directed primarily toward coaches, but I think it lays the foundation for the importance of mental training in association with physical training for all sports. Also, in a sense, I think we are all coaches on some level; if not of others, certainly at least of ourselves. This applies especially to those of us who train on our own.

Top 10 Guiding Principles for Mental Training

By Sean McCann, Ph.D., Sports Psychologist, U.S. Olympic Committee

1. Mental training can't replace physical training and talent.
We haven't seen any Olympic athlete who succeeded without doing the physical and technical work, even though we have worked with some of the most mentally talented athletes in the world. The reality is that even an exceptionally talented athlete who has not prepared well physically loses confidence and is vulnerable in competition. The best and easiest confidence is that which comes from the knowledge that you are as prepared, or more prepared, than your competitors and that you are physically capable of a winning performance.

2. Physical training and physical ability aren't enough to succeed consistently.
On the other hand, we have worked with a number of athletes whose coaches called them "the most talented athlete on the team," yet these athletes never achieved international success. These physically gifted athletes were not able to manage the mental demands of the sport. Some athletes can't handle the focus and discipline of training, and others can't handle the pressure and stress of competition. If you are lacking in either of these areas, you may succeed at times, but you will not succeed consistently.

3. A strong mind may not win an Olympic medal, but a weak mind will lose one.
It is very difficult to predict that a mentally strong athlete will win an Olympic medal, because of all the factors that play into winning a medal.

Success for any athlete is never certain; there are so many variables—training, health, finances, coaching to name a few. On the other hand, one of the easiest predictions to make is who will fail under Olympic pressure. Athletes with an obviously weak mental game virtually never win at the biggest competitions.

4. Coaches frequently don't know what their athletes are thinking.
Although all great coaches pay close attention to the behavior of their athletes on the field of play, very few have a similarly detailed knowledge of what their athletes are thinking or should be thinking.
Few coaches know enough about the specific mental "demons" athletes have, so they often are unable to intervene when they need to at competition. We have come to the conclusion that like politics or religion, it is an area many coaches are afraid to ask about. Some coaches know that "psychological factors" were the cause of an athlete failing in competition, but many of these coaches are not aware of the athlete's mental state before they compete.

5. Thoughts affect behavior. Consistency of thinking = consistency of behavior.
It is a simple but powerful idea that all sport behavior starts with a thought. Much of coaching focuses on making sport behavior more consistent and controllable, but much less of coaching focuses on making thinking more consistent and controllable. Because of this, many coaches are surprised not only by the difference between their athletes' practice behavior and competition behavior but also by the fact that the difference comes about because of how their athletes are thinking. One goal of sport psychology is to understand and control the thinking process, which will lead to understanding and control of behavior.

6. Coaches often have a different view of changing technical v. mental mistakes.
As sport psychologists, we are optimistic about the ability to work on mental mistakes. Thus we often are surprised when coaches are willing to write off an athlete as a "choker" when they repeat mental mistakes in competition. These often are the same coaches who literally will work for years with an athlete on a repeated technical mistake. To a coach who says "I don't think they'll ever do it," we ask "How many times have you worked specifically on changing the mental mistakes? What drills have you tried? How do you give athletes feedback on their mental mistakes? Do the athletes know exactly how they should think?

Have you had this discussion?"

7. Coaches must be involved in the mental training process.
In sport psychology, after a strong period of training before the season, we have heard coaches say: "Well, now it is all mental. Now it is up to the sport psychologist!" Although it is nice to feel important to a team's success, we have learned from hard experience that it is wrong for coaches to "outsource" mental training and sport psychology to a sport psychology consultant. We have learned that many elite coaches feel out of their comfort zone when dealing with mental training issues and fear asking probing questions about how an athlete thinks and feels. We also have learned to push coaches to go past their fears and get used to coaching the mental as well as the physical athlete. If coaches don't become the prime provider of sport psychology for their teams, they will miss all kinds of teaching opportunities and chances for excellence. At worst, coaches who are unaware of their athletes' mental skill-building will coach in ways that oppose or undermine the mental skills acquired. The bottom line is that coaches must be involved in mental training for it to be successful.

8. Sometimes it is okay to force athletes to take the time to do mental training.
The USOC's Sport Psychology Department's philosophy on this topic has evolved over the past 10 years. In the past, we were unwilling to say that all teams should do some form of mental training. We had been fairly passive, waiting for coaches to approach us with requests for service. Unfortunately, many of those requests came from coaches who had seen their athletes melt down in the biggest competition of their life. Obviously, it is too late at that point! Many coaches seem willing to accept an athlete's reassurance, "My mental game is just fine." Why, when you wouldn't ask athletes to determine on their own if their technique is "just fine," do you let them avoid working on their mental game for years until a crisis forces them to admit they need work? At the USOC, we are now comfortable pushing athletes into doing the mental training work, even if they don't always see the value at first.

9. Like any other skill, mental skills must be measured to maximize performance of those skills.
"What gets measured gets done." This old expression from business writer Peter Lynch is useful for coaching as well.

Just as ski coaches time their teams' training runs or basketball coaches calculate free throw shooting percentages, application of mental skills can be measured. Moreover, they must be measured if they are to change. Once you think of mental skills as behaviors to be measured, you can begin to use your own coaching creativity to teach, modify and increase the use of mental skills.

10. Coaches need to think about their own mental skills.
Most coaches readily can see that the same skills they are teaching their athletes also are useful for their own work in coaching. With the amount of pressure coaches face, use of mental skills such as the ability to manage emotions, control arousal, game plan and simulate pressure all are useful for coaches.

Now, obviously the above steps and tips are a more formal approach and can be applied to many different sports, but here is another viewpoint that is more geared towards weight training and the role of the mind therein:

Some more modern thoughts on motivation from a brief paper on Sports Psychology:

Motivation is a particularly relevant issue which can be defined as being aroused to action or to directed purposeful behavior, although this may not always be either efficient or effective (Davies, 1989). You may have noticed athletes who seem to have all of the physiological and skill components necessary for great performance, yet lack motivation, i.e. regularly show up late, do not try very hard during training etc.

Quite often, as athlete's progress in their sports, the improvements become gradually smaller. It then becomes harder for athletes to make significant improvements, and often results in a loss of motivation (Davies, 1989). An appropriate level of motivation will not only improve physical performance, it will also assist in the learning of physical skills, which in turn, will affect the quality of performance (Parker, 2000). Motivation essentially comes in two forms: Intrinsic and Extrinsic. If an athlete is motivated to perform an activity for its own sake, they are said to be intrinsically motivated. When an athlete performs an activity solely to obtain some external reward, they are extrinsically motivated. (Parker, 2000)

To improve the level of motivation in athletes the following methods could be used:

- Avoid using winning or performance outcomes, instead use the outcomes of fitness or skill
- Give Praise. All athletes need positive, honest feedback about their performances.
- Vary the content, venue and sequence of training sessions. Boredom will lead to staleness and/or burnout
- Set Goals based on the **S.M.A.R.T.E.R principle**. Goals should be specific, measurable, affirmative, realistic, time based, evaluated, and recorded. They should also be short-term, intermediate, and long term.
- Use Mental Imagery.
- Use Role-Modeling.
- A team-bonding session; when a team is bonding well, performance improves. Some training days are just hard. You show up not wanting to do your workout and think to yourself "hmmm...I'll just go a little easier today...cut some corners". Days like this are crucial. These are the days that separate the champions from the mediocre athletes. Strength and Endurance athletes have to be able to push themselves. Be strong and give your training session your best effort. After the session you'll feel a sense of accomplishment and that feeling will carry over to motivate you for future training sessions.
- Consistency. Many athletes are great at maintaining motivation for short bursts of time (a few weeks, a few months) but it is important to understand that improvements are a result of a consistent effort over a long period of time. Set some long-term goals. Where would you like to be 1 year or 3 years from now? Keeping focused on long-term goals will help you to remain consistent and not overemphasize training sessions or drive you to burnout. No one becomes his or her best overnight. It takes many years of correct practice.
- Enjoy. Remain passionate about the sport.

The 4C's

Concentration, confidence, control and commitment (the 4C's) are generally considered to be the main mental qualities that are important for successful performance in most sports.

- Concentration - This is the mental quality to focus on the task in hand. If the athlete lacks concentration then their athletic abilities will not be effectively or efficiently applied to the task. For most cycling sustained concentration is needed.
- Confidence - results from the comparison an athlete makes between the goal and their ability.
- When an athlete has self confidence they will tend to: persevere even when things are not going to plan, show enthusiasm, be positive in their approach and take their share of the responsibility in success and failure. To improve their self confidence, an athlete can use mental imagery.
- Control - ability to maintain emotional control regardless of distraction. An athlete's ability to maintain control of their emotions in the face of adversity and remain positive is essential to successful performance. Two emotions which are often associated with poor performance are anxiety and anger
    - Anxiety comes in two forms - Physical (butterflies, sweating, nausea, needing the toilet) and Mental (worry, negative thoughts, confusion, lack of concentration). Relaxation is a technique that can be used to reduce anxiety.
- Commitment - ability to continue working to agreed goals In competition with these goals the athlete will have many aspects of daily life to manage. The many competing interests and commitments include: work, studies, family/partner, friends, social life and other hobbies/sports

The techniques of relaxation and mental imagery can assist an athlete to achieve the 4C's.

The article goes on to the concepts of imagery vs. visualization, which are both useful, but the writer states that mental imagery is a step above simple visualization simply because more senses are involved. Visualization obviously is related to sight, but not the other senses. If we can take it to the level in which all the senses are activated, a deeper effect is achieved as it is more real and the memory perceives the "event" as such.

More from the article on the benefits of mental imagery:

Imagery may strengthen muscle memory, for a task, by having the muscles fire in the correct sequence for a movement, without actually executing that movement (Martin et al, 1999).

Mental Imagery can improve athletic performance without any physical activity. Mental Imagery will enhance performance if used regularly. It is seen as effective because the brain sends messages to the muscles in the body that would be used in a movement, even though the body does not actually move (Castella, 1996).

Imagery can sometimes be more effective than actual practice, because the athlete/s can visualize being in a competitive situation, and this to an extent, is more realistic and valuable. During mental rehearsal, the athlete imagines positive outcomes, and this creates a feeling of success, which in turn builds confidence (Davies, 1989).

The article finishes up with several quotes, most of which you have probably come across before:

Inspirational/Thought-Provoking Quotes

"Winners never quit and quitters never win"

"The flowers of tomorrow are the seeds of today"

"You miss 100% of the shots you never take"

"If you do what you always did, you will get what you always got"

"Tough times don't last but tough people do"

"Focus on the process, not the outcome"

The next article contains more from the realm of modern Sports Psychiatry;

Mental training involves the development of two types of skills: offensive and defensive. The mastery of offensive and defensive skills is absolutely necessary for you to be consistently successful in any form of competition. The Olympic Training Center's Sport Psychology staff has done a great deal of study on offensive and defensive mental training, and has determined that these skills can be organized into three groups: Basic Visualization ! Competition Self Talk Energy Management ! Elite Goal Setting

Lanny Bassham, 1972 Olympic Silver Medalist and 1976 Olympic Gold Medalist, has done extensive research on the subject of mental training. In his book, With Winning In Mind, he explains that performance is a function of three processes: ! Conscious Thought ! Sub-conscious Thought ! Self-Image These three processes must be balanced in order for you to perform at your maximum potential. He presents a very compelling argument for visualization by stating that the conscious mind can only think about one thing at a time. He goes on to say that the conscious is responsible for training the subconscious mind, and also for calling it into action.

Mental Training cont'd.

The subconscious can do more than one thing at a time (like walking, catching,throwing, driving, and dodging a punch), it can also cause you to shoot a perfect shot -- the same one that you have trained it to do. But what happens if you doubt your ability to shoot a center-ten? Suddenly, you cause your subconscience to follow another path -- one that does not include success. However, if you have shot many tens before, you are confident of your abilities, and are not likely to second guess them. Think about what it takes to ride a bicycle. You just get on and pedal right? You don't even have to think about it. Or do you? Once you have learned to ride a bicycle, your subconscious mind takes over. Your self-image says, "No problem. I can do this.", and your conscious mind doesn't have to put forth much effort.

However, your sub-conscious is very active: it's causing you to move your legs, adjust your balance, steer, and make thousands of other reactions and adjustments. As you can see, the conscious, sub-conscious and
self-image are very dependent upon each other. If one is too dominant, or under developed, the effect will not be as positive as having them well balanced.
Learning to shoot is like learning to ride a bike: it's a matter of balance, both physical and mental.

Visualization

See it. Feel it. Sense it. Do it.

Visualization (sometimes referred to as "Imagery" or "Rehearsal") is the first mental skill you should develop, and the most basic skill for you to rely on. It is really not much more than an active imagination that you use to guide yourself toward success. Everyone is capable of doing great things, but only those who are willing to dream about great things will actually achieve them. When you visualize, you remove the single greatest barrier between you and your success: YOU! By imagining yourself doing something great, you have taken the first step in actually doing it. Visualization is an Offensive Skill. It will help you with: Extending and increasing your training. Increasing your self-awareness. Getting you in "The Zone". Some people claim that they don't have an imagination; that they don't dream. However, studies have shown that everyone dreams, whether they remember them when they wake or not. So if you dream, you visualize.

The process of seeing success
before it happened put me in a
positive frame of mind and prepared
me to play the game.
- Michael Jordan

Visualization cont'd.

Visualization works by:
 Refining your skills
 Correcting mistakes
 Enhancing your decision making skills
Building confidence
 Dealing with adversity
 Refining concentration
 Strengthening your motivation
 Managing your emotions
 Preparing for competition
 Seeing success

Have you ever blushed at being caught talking to yourself? Almost everyone talks to themselves at some point during the day. Even if it is something simple like, "YES! I did it!" or "Oops... that's gonna hurt." Unfortunately, sometimes we say things to ourselves that can be damaging to our self image; things that would hurt our feelings if someone else said them to us. For example, if you forget to bring your shooting journal, ammunition or gun to the range you might say, "I can't believe I forgot again! I'm so *stupid*." or if you are having trouble shooting you might say somthing like, "I'm still the lowest scoring shooter on the team. I stink."

Why is it okay for you to say mean things to yourself or about yourself? It's not! After a while, you will begin to believe what you tell yourself day in and day out.

How do I fix this problem?

First of all, start by stopping. Catch yourself saying something negative, and correct it. When a negative thought enters your mind, recognize it then do something like snap your fingers or say a made up word. Then, redirect your thoughts toward what you can do to correct the things that frustrate you. If you forgot your shooting journal, then find a way to correct the problem. Write yourself a note (in your journal, of course!), and then verbally tell yourself that you will do better the next time. Picture yourself remembering. Then repeat that positive statement you just made. Every time you say something negative about yourself, say your made-up word, then repeat a positive statement twice.

Most importantly, genuinely think about what you are saying.

Self-Talk cont'd.

If you catch yourself saying the same things over and over, write down what it is that you normally say, then write down a positive way of saying it. If you normally say, "I forget everything" write something like, "I sometimes forget, but I have a plan to develop a better memory: I write things down in my journal."

Play the Pebble Game!

Something else you can do is to try putting a few pebbles in your right pants pocket when you start your day. Each time you say something negative about yourself, move a pebble from your right pocket to your left pocket. If you run out of pebbles, move all of them back to your right pocket and keep going. Make it your goal not to run out of pebbles the next day.
Once you reach that goal, throw one of the stones as far away from you as you can, like into a lake or field -- some place where you can never take back that bad habit. The pebble game is fun, but it's not magic. Just moving pebbles from one pocket to another will not change the way to think and talk to yourself. You
have to teach yourself how to say positive things to yourself and about yourself. This takes time. Don't give up, or get frustrated, and remember to reward yourself for reaching milestones and your ultimate goal: a day, week or month with only ten pebbles, five pebbles, and even NO PEBBLES in your pockets! Track your goals using your journal, and a Goal Plan worksheet.

Just say, "Thank you."

Always accept a compliment! It has become fashionable with women to be unfashionable. Have you ever heard one woman say, "What a lovely dress!" Only to hear the recipient of that compliment reply, "This old thing?"

It's a running gag in Hollywood, but it's one that is sure to make you choke when it comes to reaching your goals. Most people don't hand out free compliments. That makes compliments very valuable, so accept them whenever possible. Just say, "Thank you." And accept the compliment. You will reinforce your self image, and best of all, you will do it gracefully without appearing too modest or too vain.

Shoot More Tens!

Another important thing to remember is to figure out what you are doing right on the good shots, then figure out what you can do to repeat that success. Avoid getting angry or frustrated with your performance, and don't try to figure out why some of your shots are not as good as others.

Choose Good Friends!
Be careful who you associate with. Choose your friends wisely, and avoid people who speak negatively about themselves or others. The same principle applies to people who talk about their bad scores and poor performances. Walk away from them, and don't look back. Find someone who will inspire you and challenge you with positive words and encouragement.

Don't Forget Your Successes

The Shooting Sports ETC curriculum has a form for you to use to record your accomplishments. It does not have a form for you to record your failures. Be sure to record your successes and achievements whenever they occur, and forget about everything else.

(The above is obviously directed at the shooting sports, but the concepts apply universally, I think)

And some more;

On Mental Toughness

Department of Human Movement and Exercise Science, University of Western Australia. Scott Cresswell has a Masters degree in Sport Psychology from the University of Otago in New Zealand. He is an accredited Sport Psychology Consultant and contracted to the New Zealand Academy of Sport and is currently researching player burnout for the New Zealand Rugby Union.

What is mental toughness?

Mental toughness refers to a player's psychological skills that are advantageous to performance. But what are these skills? One way to begin thinking about psychological skills is to think of a player that you admire for their on-field ability. Ask yourself - "What mental characteristics make that player stand out?" For example, some attributes might be a player's concentration under pressure, motivation to train/perform or confidence.

Can mental toughness be taught?

Mental toughness is often referred to in everyday conversations as an elusive quality possessed by only a few elite sportspeople. On the contrary, it is the view of people working in sport psychology that psychological skills can be taught. While psychological skills themselves are often talked about, the psychological methods used to enhance these skills are not as well known. Often, players have developed some of these skills through experience and also through trial and error. Over time they tried different techniques and adopted those that worked and modified those that did not. Practical sport psychology is about developing mental toughness by teaching and practicing proven methods with players and coaches. Sport psychology has several goals for teaching these mental skills, including enhancing performance and increasing enjoyment. Some of the more well-known methods for enhancing mental skills for sport include goal setting, self-talk and imagery. Elements of a mental toughness program can be as simple as developing a set routine of physical and mental preparation designed to get a player ready (physically and mentally) before a game and when returning to the field after half-time. This routine could involve going over key tasks as they will need to be performed on the field both in your mind (for example using imagery and self-talk) and physically.

How much time should a player spend on mental skills?

The amount of time that players should spend on their mental toughness will vary depending on how important they feel it is for their performance. One way to ensure a player has an appropriate balance in his training is for the player to ask him/herself – "How much time do I spend training my body for competition (e.g. fitness, skills, strength)?" Then ask him/herself – "How much time do I spend training my mind for competition (e.g. motivation, confidence, concentration)?" Despite the role that aspects such as concentration and confidence play in achieving their best performance, the majority of players find they spend far more time training physically, neglecting the mental aspects of their performance. This does not mean that a player should train mental skills more than physical skills, but it does mean that mental skills should be given some consideration.

What can I do as a coach?

Often, one of the most effective ways a sport psychology professional can assist a team is by consulting with the coach. As the readership of this magazine is primarily coaches, I have decided to focus on two coaching strategies that impact on the mental toughness of players.

Strategy one - Open and honest communication.

In my research, rugby players have expressed a desire for open and honest communication. Within any team environment, coaches face challenges that, if not handled appropriately, may result in negative outcomes for the individual players and/or the team. In rugby this issue often has to do with selection. Players often feel threatened in the rugby environment if they are not selected. If the reasons for non-selection are not explained clearly, players can lose confidence (i.e. decreased mental toughness) in their ability and the coach. Poor communication can lead to a perception of unfair treatment and leave players feeling undervalued, a motivated and isolated whilst losing trust and respect for the coach. While good communication is often acknowledged as a valuable team asset and is a core value in many team environments, many coaches are still unsure on how to facilitate it. Some key guidelines for coaches when communicating with players are:

☐ *Plan the points you want to get across.*
This will help ensure your message is easy to follow.

☐ *Keep it simple.*
Often, three new things are as much as someone can contemplate at once.

Overload will result in a lost message.

Stick to the relevant information. For example, a player could be confused after discussing his non-selection with a coach if many more positive, rather than negative,
aspects of the player's performance were discussed.

☐ *Provide opportunities for players to communicate their concerns.*

☐ *Encourage player feedback and participation*. This often helps to facilitate understanding.

☐ *Build understanding.* Share perspectives with players. Enhancing their understanding of
your concerns may help them to empathise with your point of view and vice versa.

☐ *Address the problem not the player*. Make sure any criticism is directed towards the
player's actions rather than him personally.

Strategy two - competition simulation. Simulating competition situations and pressure is a key strategy to build a player's mental toughness. Confidence primarily comes from physical practice because it provides a player with the knowledge that he has successfully completed the task in the past. Coaches can help facilitate this by simulating the pressure situations. For example, many coaches advocate running players through drills such as three attackers on two defending players in a limited space, forcing ad-hoc decision-making and execution. While simulating pressure is common within some training environments, coaches can extend this to other possible situations, such as goal kicking, playing with a man down, defensive live scrimmaging and practicing with a proper referee. The key is to make the situations as real as possible.

What about individual player skills?

Players can work on psychological skills individually. Psychological skills can be enhanced by using a number of different methods, such as imagery, self-talk and goal setting as mentioned earlier. Covering all of these is beyond the scope of my comment here. An example of a method that can help individuals to build mental toughness is self-talk.

Self-talk simply refers to the things that players say to themselves inside their head while they are playing. Self-talk can be simple skill instructions. For example, a goal kicker may say, "Head down, follow through," to his/her self just prior to taking a kick in order to focus on the technique of the kick rather than the importance of the outcome. In the same situation a goal kicker may say, "I have kicked from this distance thousands of times before," to his/her self to promote confidence prior to taking an important kick.

What about team mental toughness?

There are also certain attributes that make some teams mentally tougher than other teams. For example, some teams have a high ability to work well together under pressure. Team work is often referred to in sport psychology as the **task cohesion** of a group. There is also another dimension to cohesion - social cohesion - or, how well players get on together in social situations. Task cohesion, however, is often the primary concern of coaches as it relates more directly to on-field performance. There are several ways that coaches can build task cohesion. For example, doing tasks that require good communication and understanding among players on the field is one way to help facilitate task cohesion. These team activities not only help the team, they can also benefit an individual player's confidence and motivation.

While we are on the topic of "mental Toughness", here is another take on it, from elitefts site;

I love training and building up my physique. For twenty years, I was extremely consistent. My goal was to get as massive as possible. I was never a bodybuilder— I just trained like one. However, I always felt something was missing. I could never pinpoint what I was lacking with my lifting, but I definitely felt there was a certain emptiness to it. About eight years ago, I stumbled upon a book written by coach John Davies. I felt a strong connection to the "renegade training" philosophy he created. His system was more than just lifting or building muscles. The heart of renegade training was about being mentally tough. It was a whole cerebral system about seeking challenges and overcoming adversity. It was about honor. I finally knew what was missing in my twenty years of training—the mental aspect. Coach Davies really had a strong impact on me and made me question how and why I was training. I was always building muscles and mass, but I never thought of the psychological aspect.

I knew my training was making me physically more attractive, but besides looking good, I didn't see how my training made me mentally stronger. Training was supposed to make you feel more confident, but being self-assured wasn't always my strong point. At different stages in my life, I would say I was mentally weak and gave into fear. At other points of my life, I could be a fighter with a very strong sense of will who would stubbornly refuse to quit. I was inconsistent with activating my will and desire. I never realized that perseverance was a skill one can learn. I soon became obsessed with other mental toughness teachers like Lombardi, "miracle on ice coach" Herb Brooks, and wrestling great Dan Gable. Through grueling work, perseverance can be taught. Mental toughness training isn't for everyone, but it should be. It is needed. Without mental toughness, one is always vulnerable for a breakdown no matter how big you are or how good you look.

An interesting pattern

I've been a member of Gold's Gym in Venice for almost 30 years and the old World Gym that Joe Gold used to own. In that time, I've seen massively huge people over the years come and go at both places. When I first joined those gyms in the 1980s, I saw guys and gals in their bulking up stage bigger than you can ever imagine. I'm not talking about the pros like Tom Platz, Ferrigno, and even Arnold that I would see regularly. It was the amateurs that I was most impressed with. Some of these guys came out of nowhere and were up to a hundred pounds bigger than the pros. They would make your jaw drop if you saw these exaggerated masses of muscles. Most of the time, I thought for sure some of these no-name colossal monsters would be the next world champion bodybuilders. However, to my surprise, just a couple of them ever won anything significant. Some of the hard luck amateurs continued to beef it up and train at the gym, but after losing a contest, the majority of them withered away and then disappeared. You would constantly hear stories about how some of these big monsters would shrink back to their normal size when they got off the drugs, become fat and out of shape, and then vanish from the face of the earth. I'm not picking on bodybuilders either. Living 30 years in Los Angles, the home of broken dreams, I've seen weekend warriors, models, and actors who were in shape and great looking fall apart from the constant disappointment and rejection. Some survive and continue pursuing their dreams, but others never recover from the cruel pain of adversity associated with the pursuit of stardom. For those who can't handle the hardship, unfortunately a long and horrible road of self-destruction can be the norm. So it doesn't matter how beautiful or big you are.

If you're mentally weak, you will always be vulnerable to a mental collapse. I refuse to ever be that weak again. Through hard work, discipline, and dedication, I have changed my mind set.

New goals

As I approached turning 40, I was overweight and had developed hypertension. I now had a new goal for my training—to be mentally stronger than ever. I started reading about how effective Crossfit was and reluctantly started to incorporate classes once a week. In all my years of bulking up, I never did any cardio. The only aerobics I did was reading the sports page while pedaling very slowly on the bike machine. Most of the Crossfit workouts were heavily cardio oriented, so I struggled. Boy, did I struggle. The workouts always seemed like a competitive race, and except one time when that pregnant lady was in my class, I was always the last one to finish. Yet, there was something new and exciting about this weekly training adventure. Most people develop their mental toughness through playing a sport. However, I wasn't a very good athlete growing up and never played many. With Crossfit, I was experiencing real physical competition for the first time and I loved it. Humiliated by past failures on the playground and now reliving the shame in these Crossfit classes, I defiantly took a stance. I was tired of getting my ass kicked. I pushed myself harder than I ever thought my body could take. As physically fatigued as I was during the workout, my mind was not tired. It was stimulated. I pushed my body to be aggressive and relentless in the workouts. I had no idea what the hell I was doing or where I was getting this new level of determination and strength. In retrospect, I was learning how to activate my will. I was making the connection with my thoughts and letting my mind lead my body. I started to crush my times and finish not only first but way ahead of everyone else. Nobody was more shocked than I was at my sudden athleticism in my early 40s. I felt a sense of confidence after the workouts that I never had before. Unfortunately, it was short lived and my strut didn't transfer over when I was at a singles bar. I give Crossfit all the credit for getting me in the best shape of my life by pushing me to a level that I just didn't realize existed. Through all the suffering, I started to see how vital the mental aspect of training was for me. Everybody else was stronger, faster, and more athletic than I was, but I felt now I had the advantage. I knew I was mentally stronger than everyone else in the class.

The main job of Crossfit is to get you in bad ass shape. It did its job and beyond for me. However, like my bodybuilding workouts, I needed something more than just a physical challenge.

The greatest strength of all

There was nothing out there that fed my mental hunger, so I started to create my own workouts with the priority to challenge my mind first. I didn't come up with a new system. In fact, I went back in time and did traditional full body strength workouts and said goodbye to the isolation work that dominated my first twenty years of training. I continued to do Crossfit and Krav Maga and kept on doing things that I hated and sucked at like running and climbing rope. Over the past three years, my emphasis in the gym was to get physically stronger. But more importantly, I have been stronger in my personal life. Knowing you can get over any adversity is the greatest strength of all.

Problems of teaching mental toughness

I started to become very obsessed with addressing the mental game. I read as many articles and books as possible. The problem is most of the literature out there is for professional athletes. But the biggest problem with just about all the mental toughness training I've seen is the emphasis on lame positive affirmations. Telling yourself you're a fighting machine over and over again is just a waste of time and creates a false sense of security. You can say these positive affirmations until you're blue in the face, but once you have to throw down in an octagon, it's more than likely you will get your teeth kicked in.

Other techniques in the strange world of mental toughness training are self-hypnoses and subliminal tapes, and for thousands of dollars, you can try altering brain wave machines. I'm not making this stuff up. Professional athletes will pay mega dollars to improve their mental game. The problem is there isn't any easy way or short cut to teaching toughness. Mental toughness is not for sale. The only way to get mentally tougher is by earning it. The second half of this bad news is that you pretty much have to go through some pretty awful shit to earn it, too. It won't be fun and it's going to hurt. I wish there was an easier method to toughening up your mind, but only through suffering can one truly learn character issues that can't be taught any other way. But it's well worth it. This doesn't mean you have to give up your current bodybuilding or conditioning workouts. Adding the mental aspects to your training can be very easy. Training your mind and body should go hand in hand. Everyone wants to be mentally tougher but not everyone wants to pay the price for it. The number one factor that will determine if you will become psychologically stronger is your determination. For me, I didn't want it. I needed it. If you understand this statement, you have what it takes.

Tips to help you incorporate mental toughness

Tip #1: You must believe perseverance is a skill. Like any skills, perseverance can be honed in, practiced, and strengthened. Think of perseverance like a muscle. The more you work it, the stronger it will get. If you don't use it, it will shrivel up. If this all sounds too elusive, think of perseverance as your will. Your will is the imposing of your desire into behavior. The more determined your will is, the less likely you will give up. One of the best ways to practice activating your will is when you work out. Get your will involved in your workout as much as possible. For example, if you're doing bicep curls and are struggling with the last reps, instead of feeling "the pump" of your muscles, engage your will. See how many more reps you get by mentally willing yourself to do more. It's a slight distinction to what you already do. However, you want to give more credit to your will for doing the hard stuff than your body parts. Your will is your power. A strong will can lead you to extraordinary things or get you out of a terrible situation. Through constant testing and practice, you can have a better connection with your will.

Tip #2: There is a direct relationship with your mental toughness training in the gym and with your personal life. Too many people separate their training from what they do in the gym and how they live. They categorize their strength to only what they can do in the gym. They are very strong with the bench press but are pushovers in their relationships. They have huge arms but are mentally fragile.

They don't see the connection with how physical strength training can improve mental power. With mental fitness training, you want to see the connection with what you do in the gym and how you live your life. The strength you feel at the gym should carry over to your inner strength when you have a job interview or the blind date that your co-worker has set you up with. Your confidence should rise across the board and not only after you bench press. And vice versa—how you handle getting over an awful ordeal in your life should make the animal in you come out the next time you have to do a brutal workout. There should be no separation between the activation of your will and the situation. Your will is blind and indifferent to the circumstances that you will face. It does not discriminate between how much mental strength you must draw on for you to set a personal record with the bench press and what you must do to get out of life-threatening situations. Your will responds by doing the same thing for either situation. It will overcome the challenge with aggressive and relentless actions. This aggression does not mean you must be high strung or frantic. On the contrary, you must be methodical and focus with complete determination. You are on a mission with only one goal—to get out of the mess you're in. You want your will to be available and ready to be called upon immediately—anywhere and at all times. You want to train your will not to distinguish who your opponent is. Its only concern is to whip out the enemy with fierce tenacity. This is the aggressive mind frame you need when you walk on to the playing field and when you walk out to face the unpredictable cruelest of these games—life.

Tip 3: You must learn to do what is uncomfortable for you. To develop the psychological edge, you must have extreme discipline to give up the comfort zone that you train and live in. Delaying immediate satisfaction is the ultimate sacrifice that all warriors must choose. Think of it this way—a young baby's world is about the instant gratification that it seeks. All addicts failed at delaying gratification. Overeating is a sign for those needing instant pleasure. The feeble mind is all about the immature joys of the now without any regard for the long term. To develop mental hardness, you must learn to do what the weak general population has failed to do. You must delay the temptation of immediate gratification for the rewards of the long haul. To separate yourself from the norm, you must put yourself in an uncomfortable state. And you must do this often; very often. And I'm not talking about watching the whole first season of "Golden Girls" with your mother in-law either. Going to the gym is one the best ways to practice being in a physical state of misery. Challenge your tolerance to mental anguish by once a week doing a high intensity anaerobic workout. The best thing about high intensity anaerobic workouts is that each set should last less than two minutes.

They also give your testosterone hormones a boost, so you'll build muscle. The down side of high intensity workouts is that you literally learn what it feels like to *almost* die. Twenty rep squats, extended drops sets, and breathing squats are all classic, old school brutal anaerobic workouts and avoided by today's contemporary pansy gym rats. However, it they want something hip to kick their ass, Crossfit is the newest trend. One of my favorite Crossfit workouts is called Fran. I like the simplicity of this workout because it combined two compound movements into one metabolic session. You load 95 pounds on a barbell and superset barbell squats with an overhead press with pull-ups—three sets of 21, 15, and 9 reps in the quickest time possible. This means that if you want to be an elite bad ass, you won't have much time to rest. You can get big and ripped by doing this workout *if you survive* the extreme breathlessness. If you do Fran correctly, you should want to puke. If not, you didn't crank up the intensity enough so you better have a good vomit the next time. If you want to test your perception of being a bad ass, Fran is a good place to start. Another simple but brutal anaerobic workout is the Litvonvi workout. Created by Dan John after the methods of a Russian hammer thrower, I highly suggest the Litvonvi for those who fear cardio work will make them lose muscle. You might go into cardiac arrest from this workout, but you won't burn muscle because it will increase testosterone and HGH production. Like Fran, with the Litvonvi you'll gain muscle and mental toughness points *if* you finish the workout. Basically, you do six reps of heavy front squats followed by a 400-meter run or 100-yard dash. Three sets and that's it. Sounds easy but this workout is extremely vicious. My reaction the first time I did the Litvinov workout was "God, help me." It was by far the hardest workout I've ever done. Having a strong will is crucial for you to get through these gruesome workouts. If you have no connection with your will, you will drown. The fatigue that your body will feel will be excruciating. Just remember, just because your body is fatigued doesn't mean you mind has to be tired. Will your body to be aggressive and relentless in the face of exhaustion.

Learning to be mentally energetic when your body is weak is a sign of an indomitable will. Now if this all sounds too intimidating, six sets of hill sprints is a fine substitute. As long as the anaerobic workout can cause mayhem and havoc on you mentally, it has done its job. The good news is that the suffering that you go through isn't all that bad. Physically, you should feel spent, but emotionally finishing the gruesome workouts should be fulfilling. You should feel a great sense of accomplishment after you make it through the workouts. Mentally toughness training is accumulative. Each victory builds upon each other. Mental conditioning in the gym is only half of the process.

Like how you need to overcome discomfort in your physical tests, you also have to confront the emotional stress in your personal life, too. Make a list of things you have been avoiding or problems that you have a difficult time getting over. We avoid confronting these issues because of they pain they cause us. However, the more we deny these negative issues, the more they have the potential to destroy us. We sit back and wish they go away, but they don't. We become passive due to the fear that we overwhelmingly feel. Fear is a needed quality to develop mental strength. By facing fear, you learn courage. Being fearless is a misconceived trait. As admirable as being fearless can be, it isn't realistic nor does it provide any benefit to being a mentally tough beast. Being threatened by fear is the catalyst for you to strike! Confronting fear with brave actions is how you get tough. Fear is an emotional response. At times, fear is irrational and blown out of perspective. It is not easy getting over any shattering experiences, but with guts and determination, you can get over any painful ordeal. Life is full of disappointments and letdowns. When we don't get what we want, the consolation is that we gain experience. This doesn't seem like a worthwhile prize, but see how the adversity can enlighten you. If may not be obvious, but look hard at any opportunity for personal growth. Take in the life lesson and move on. So despite being in the gym or your personal situation, a tough mental standoff in either circumstance will affect both aspects of your life. Your goal is to be mentally invincible *regardless* of where you are.

Tip #4: You are your worst enemy. As you begin the journey to empower your mind, you will be constantly tested. Your worst enemy will not be your competition. Unfortunately, you will be low balled the most by yourself. Your body will attempt to look for an escape route for what it sees as unnecessary pain it has to go through. For me, the actual physical pain wasn't the most daunting part of the training. The anticipation of it was the hardest part. Hours before the workout, I would be mentally drained. To relieve myself of this self-imposed psychological torture, my mind would begin to procrastinate and look for excuses not to do the workout. I would always come up with logical reasons or lies on why I should ditch the workout. It is a mental chess game between you and yourself. It is your job to decipher the truth and lies. What is true is that mental toughness training isn't easy and that's the way it must be. You are preparing yourself for the worst case scenario. The pain you are feeling is nothing like the cruelties that life offers us. Feel lousy now so you can be stronger tomorrow. This is the sick logic of those who are in the mentally tough club. You will hear many negative thought patterns often during your trial of cerebral improvement. Learn to change the negative thought pattern into positive self-talk. So instead of saying, "I've got three more sets to go. I can't do this;" say "I'm getting mentally stronger.

I did five sets so three more sets will be easy for me." Learn to change the negativism to something reachable and specific with a possible solution. So instead of saying something cynical like, "I'll never find a job again!" change it to something positive like, "If I spend two hours on monster.com, I know I should fill out at least five job applications." Mental toughness is all about your thought process. Your thoughts can make you do what most would consider unconceivable. This is what this training is all about.

Your journey to mental toughness

In conclusion, we all work hard at the gym so we can build the best bodies and become as physically strong as possible. Being mentally tougher can help sustain all the work you put in to improve your body and strength. More importantly, being mentally tough can help improve your quality of life. It is a very challenging adventure but a worthwhile one. Good luck with your journey.

Here is an excerpt from Critical Bench's 50 Ways to a bigger bench that says it well:

Attitude

"**You have to visually see yourself locking the weight out.**" If you've successfully completed the movement over and over in your mind prior to the lift, nothing will stop you. "**Attitude is everything**" and will always be the most important tool you have. Your attitude can take you to places and open doors others thought impossible. That's what makes the difference between a champion lifter and an average lifter. Attitude takes you beyond your potential. Apply a positive attitude from the time you get up in the morning to your final thought before you retire at night. Attitude can reach deep into your soul causing an adrenaline rush taking you to unbelievable heights of success. **Push your attitude before, during and after training, and the weight will increase.**
–700 Pound Bencher Mark Carter

I recently was reading some of Dave Draper's wit and wisdom from his Iron online website. The following quote is a good example of Dave's musings and kind of sums up why consistency is needed:

Dave Draper

"There are basically two types of people who use weight training for fitness. Type A, the driven and type B, the not-so-driven. Though the degrees of difference vary, I know that for those of you of the A type, it would be an act of cruelty to keep you from your workout - an absolute impossibility, like stopping the movement of a glacier or the stampede of wild horses. And then there are amongst you of the B type, neither lazy nor irresponsible, who can't seem to make it to the gym (or the garage) on a regular basis. You have a long list of reasons why you can't and some of them are even pretty good. It is to this larger half of the population to whom I speak. To be effective, exercise must be consistent. This is the first and foremost precept of physical conditioning. If there's a secret, it's consistency. Don't quote me on this, but I believe bad exercise, badly executed consistently is far better than no exercise at all. Getting to the gym whether you want to or not, even for a short appearance, a salute or a bow is vitally important to the health of your fitness lifestyle. A break in consistency leads to the erosion of your training foundations, and without sound foundations no structure will stand. How do we train consistently, especially if we don't have a milligram of discipline or patience? To be consistent, training must be desirable, not drudgery, not dull, boring or fruitless. It must and can be exciting. I bought my first set of weights when I was ten years old, haven't put them down since, and still find them fun and fulfilling. (Embarrassing - that I don't have any brains has nothing to do with it!) For training to be productive, you must look forward to it with enthusiasm and confidence. Merely doing it is not good enough. Train with steady pace, moving from set to set, breathing fully to oxygenize and psychologically prepare for the set to follow. Get involved with the flow of your exercise, always focused on your immediate task and surroundings. Concentrate on the muscle's action, the burn, the pump, the extension and contractions. This is not advanced thinking reserved for champions and pros. No time is too soon to think in these terms. If you're brand new in the gym, practicing your exercises with these obscure thoughts in mind will speed your progress.

Always keep your eye on your goal, knowing you'll eventually achieve it and savor the time spent along the way. Absence is erosive. In fact, your presence in the gym can be restoring, even bring you out of depression, solve a problem, squash stress or inspire you to have the best workout of your life. Try it! Just go to the gym when all roads lead elsewhere, maybe nowhere. I've discovered new exercise angles, approaches and combinations on these very low energy, low spirited times out of simple instinct and survival. I can't count how many times people have crawled in the front door of our World Gyms in Santa Cruz, a slim smile pasted on their face and 30 heroic minutes later march out exclaiming *"I made it!"* Basically, you'll want to settle into a sound exercise program for at least 6-8 weeks to provide your mind with order and discipline. It also provides time to understand each exercise separately and collectively and to afford the healthy overload to the muscles so they respond by growing strong."

I really can appreciate Dave's thoughts, and he is right on the money, I think.

Some more Old School wisdom from John Grimek on the subject:

The Mental Approach

by John Grimek (1961)

One of Grimek's many great training articles

One fact appears to be certain in the weight lifting field: **whenever anyone fails to make substantial gains from training, he immediately begins to search for some nonexistent secrets that will assure him of success.** He feels that he must find these hidden techniques if he is to attain his physical goal. Do they exist?

If you mean certain magic-like special exercises, or super result-producing combinations of repetitions and sets, or a diet that will guarantee extraordinary results for all who follow it, then the answer is, they do not exist. **But there is one often overlooked aspect of training that affects and controls one's improvement, and this is the trainee's psychological approach to training.** Undoubtedly a number of you have found yourselves wondering why some fellows seem to make faster improvement than others. An obvious answer, and one which applies in many cases, is simply that nature has provided certain individuals with bodies which are more receptive to the stimulation of exercise than others. Most bodybuilders and lifters share this opinion. **But there is more to it than this**. The average lifter instinctively seems to sense this, but when asked about it is never quite able to put his finger on it. He knows an explanation does exist, but hasn't the vaguest idea what that explanation is, and hence the answer must be that it is a "secret." In trying to figure out why some gain quickly and others not at all or only slightly, we must not lose sight of all the factors involved. For instance, how does the individual train? What method of training does he follow? And **most important of all, what is his mental outlook in relation to exercise? The latter statement is especially important because it acts as a direct force in helping him to reach his goal if he steers it properly.** I realize that this statement may not impress you at this time, and you may, with some skepticism, ask yourself what's so important about one's mental approach. The answer is – **EVERYTHING**! Does this answer surprise you? Does it raise doubts in your mind? If so, don't fret, because many who haven't given this matter any thought find it hard to accept. **It's true, nevertheless, when one has the proper psychological approach it bolsters his desires and intensifies his drive, gives him that extra energy he may need to reach his goal. Moreover, the right attitude is equally as important as selecting the right training system.** Let's delve into the subject more fully. Let us take two fellows with equal physical qualities and who are following identical training systems. One of them, however, feels that he will not accomplish ANYTHING by employing this method so goes about it listlessly. The other one greatly favors and believes in it and tackles his training more zestfully.

It's easy to guess, from this description, which of the two will make outstanding gains. It's safe to say, too, that the one who likes his training will, in all probability, make three to five times the improvement of the other fellow, simply because he believes in his efforts. Of course, it's natural for one to conclude, under the circumstances, that this lack of improvement is solely due to his failure to put "his all" in his training. And this is correct up to a point. The fact remains, however, that because his mental approach is so impotent and lackadaisical he can't push himself to an all-out effort. It acts like a psychological block that prevents him from enjoying such training, dampens his spirit and restricts his physical output. **Such individuals subconsciously accept a defeatist attitude and become mentally depressed, thus voiding the possible benefits that may accrue from their efforts. You must learn to recognize that a vast difference exists between those who know that their training will benefit them, and those who feel it is utterly useless.** It is also true that those who enjoy their training will invariably benefit from it because they seem to train harder. So it's plain to see how much one's mental approach works. But the question of interest to you is, no doubt, how does this affect you? I'll try to explain by saying that when your mental attitude is optimistic about training it helps to bring you within easier reach of your goal than when your outlook is pessimistic. For this reason you should **aim towards the pinnacle of success and not at the halfway mark.** And with your mental facilities all geared up you shouldn't have any trouble attaining your ultimate aim and I intend no pun with the phrase 'all geared up' here. Along this line let me mention a very striking example of the strong psychological approach – that grand old timer, Maxick. If anyone had the power of mental control in relation to strength, he did. It's been said many times that he would go into deep concentration after each training session when he wanted to accomplish a specific lift or some unusual feat of strength.

Never once did he recognize defeat, or that he would fail in his objective.

Maxick

His thoughts always dwelled on the positive outcome of his training labors, and that he would perform the feat he desired when the time came . . . and he always did. Another outstanding example of this type was **Tony Terlazzo,** former world and Olympic champion. He also maintained a positive mental approach. Weeks before a contest he would affix certain poundage in his mind which he hoped to succeed with, and then he trained towards that goal. There were times when he overshot himself, again no pun intended, that's true, but he realized that in order to lift progressively heavier weights he must etch these poundage upon his mind so they would not frighten him when the time came to lift them. Eventually he got so far ahead of everyone in his class that he would often try to lift a higher total than those in a heavier division, and often succeeded.

The whole idea proved to be a terrific incentive that forced him far ahead of his competitors and made him the champion that he was.

Figure 6. A classical Maxick's pose showing his marvellous abdominal development.

Terlazzo

Of course even he could not have forged so far ahead had it not been for his positive mental approach to training and competing. But he was one of the very few to recognize this principle and used it to advantage. **Tommy Kono**, the present world and Olympic champion, also uses this positive approach in his lifting. "**Think big and you'll lift big**" is his motto. And he's proved this point by making world records and making and winning many world lifting titles. Had he embraced a defeatist attitude instead of a positive one I doubt if the lifting world would have heard of him at all. Now do you believe that your mental approach is important?

Tommy Kono

In a small way the foregoing should help to explain why records in all sports are higher today than they were 15 to 20 years ago. For one thing, athletes have to prepare themselves mentally to shoot for these higher marks, consequently they approach them with greater confidence <u>than if they didn't adopt such lofty aims.</u>

More on Maxick:

Before I began researching for and writing this book, I had come across the name of Maxick but was not well versed in his methods or his philosophies, but the mention here by Grimek stirred my interest again. I found a book about him which contained a lot of excerpts from his training programs, as well as those of some of his students that became great practitioners of his ideas. I think I had kind of written him off as being in the same realm as Charles Atlas, pushing a strictly non-weight exercise agenda because it was a great venue from which to derive a profitable mail-order business because expensive equipment was not required. In doing the research for my books "Forgotten Secrets of the Old-time Strongmen" and "King Squat, Rise to Power", I learned about Alan Calvert, the founder of Philadelphia's Milo Barbell, and his rivalry with the likes of Maxick. Calvert, of course, claimed that true strength and power required barbells being lifted and that there was no comparison between the results of barbell based training and self resistance or a muscle control based program. In reality, Maxick himself was one of the strongest weightlifters of his time, though his frequency of training with weights was minimal when compared to that of other good lifters of the era. Maxick was a sickly child and found himself physically inferior to his peers when he was finally able to attend school. Because of his frail condition, his parents did not condone any real strenuous exertion, and would have been unable to afford barbells or the like because of their financial state anyway. Young Max was bound and determined to find some way of changing his physical condition for the better, especially in regard to his strength or lack thereof. It was this predicament that lead him to devise the system of self resistance and muscle control that he did, according to his own reports, and the system was not his own version of someone else's pre-existing program. He had to learn to use mind over matter and to become intimately familiar with the connection between the mind and the muscles. I think the Maxalding program was/is far superior to that of Charles Atlas and others.

It is not a quickly learned art, consisting merely of a handful of exercises in which one muscle opposes another and the pose is held for a brief period. Maxick & Saldo's version goes quite a bit deeper than that. There are some muscle groups and individual muscles that are very tough to flex or tense up simply by an act of the will and without using some form of external resistance, yet according to Maxick's writings, when & if one practiced and studied enough in his system, they could control these muscles that way. Max wrote of the need to become very familiar with all the individual muscles of the body and their actions, and then to learn to control their every action with the power of the mind. The development of the powers of the will was not just the means to an end, but an end in itself. This ability enables one to be successful in just about every area of life, not just in strength training. Self confidence is built up through practice and applies to all aspects of life. It is interesting to note that Max would describe himself as not being all that "keen" when it came to lifting weights, but that his mind over muscle abilities enabled him to be a world-class lifter. He said that he only lifted weights in order to prove that muscle control was the biggest and most important factor in the ability to perform feats of strength. Maxick was even more concerned with overall health issues and claimed that one could very strongly positively affect the inner workings of the body through the powers he ascribed to. Max did readily admit that one would have to do some weight training in order to lift maximal poundage, and it could not be achieved simply through the self resistance and muscle control methods. Maxick, like many others mentioned in this book, reiterated over and over again that the first step to becoming strong is DESIRE. It is all about wanting it badly enough. A burning desire is that key starting point to truly achieve great things, and with it, many obstacles can be overcome. Max Sick's abilities were legendary. One of his incredible feats of strength was to lie on a platform and tense his abdominal area while a 180-200 pound man would jump from a 7 foot platform onto his stomach, bouncing off it as if it was a trampoline. Don't try this at home! He said that strength in its essence is a **condition of consciousness**, and that all forms of exercises, regardless of if weights, bodyweight or self-resistance are used are just means to an end.

He said further that the mind is the origin and real instrument of strength development. Max said that weights do offer certain advantages in training, one of which is tendon strengthening, which is not well afforded through muscle poses alone. He also freely admitted that learning to control and strengthen the muscles has a shorter learning curve than when using on external resistance at all. It is fascinating to note that a famous anatomist of his day said that Maxick, through his tremendous mental discipline of his body, was actually able to surpass his physical limitations. **Edward Aston** was a peer of Maxick's and competed with him in weightlifting. He was a great admirer and respecter of Max's and used some of Max's training ideas for his own betterment in Physical Culture. Aston reiterated the absolute importance of the role of proper attitude in physical training and development. Going through the motions of an exercise, no matter how sound the form of the exercise or how precisely executed, would be futile if the mind was not focused on the task. I have seen countless folks in the gym mindlessly performing some rote routine, but obviously with their minds in some other place. While I can't say this is completely useless, it is of far less value than a workout during which one's attention was focused like a laser on every rep of every set. This is the biggest determiner of progress and success in a training program, yet somehow often gets overlooked by those engaged in it. Every great bodybuilder, lifter, runner or successful athlete of any kind will confirm just how utterly important a positive attitude is in achieving great things. As the mind believes, so the body achieves. If you think you can't do a thing, you surely will be unable to do it, but conversely, if you firmly believe you can do something, you will eventually be able to do it. You will simply persist in your positive thoughts, beliefs and efforts until the thing has been done. There is nothing magical about this; this is just how things work in the real world. As the avid fan of all things Old-School in terms of physical strength training that I have become in recent years, I have learned that the primary factor which enabled men to lift the weights, develop the physiques and perform the incredible feats of strength that they did without the use of any performance enhancing substances was the role of the mind and the attitude.

It is a shame that in our current day many trainees have sought the chemical shortcuts to quick gains and have completely bypassed the training of the mind which is of even greater value than simply popping a pill or injecting something into one's rear-end. Besides that, the mental training which brings about physical excellence brings with it a host of other benefits that are useful in many other, if not all aspects of life. This certainly cannot be said of performance enhancing drugs, and in fact the use of these very likely will detract from many other areas of one's life other than strength or muscle building. Maxick seems to have been one of the most successful users of **visualization** that ever lived. I think he took this to an unprecedented level and it was what made the difference between him and those that would come later, espousing a watered down version of what he did, with systems called "isotension", vibro-power, The Atlas program and others. I would venture to say that self resistance, isometric exercise, and muscle tensing done without the accompanying visualization techniques as developed and used by Maxick and Saldo would be of far less value, and this is why these methods have fallen into dis-favor in the larger strength seeking community. Many have written off their abilities (Maxick, Saldo and some of their students) as stemming from some innate inborn quality that only they had and no other, or at least very few others would be able to duplicate by using their training methods. Maxick spoke of his going to bed at night with the thought of waking up a stronger man the next morning, constantly feeding himself strong positive thoughts about performing at a higher level with each ensuing training session. He talked about "paying the price" of total devotion to one's cause in order to excel at it. **Perseverance** is of primary importance.

Along these lines, I just ran across an interesting note from one of the greats of the NFL:

"**Confidence comes from hours and days and weeks and years of constant work and dedication. When I'm in the last two minutes of a December playoff game, I'm drawing confidence from wind sprints I did the previous March. It's just a circle: work and confidence, then more work and more confidence.**" - Roger Staubach

Maxick said that nothing becomes a reality that has not first been thoroughly visualized as a reality in the mind. Actions are preceded by thoughts, and of course, positive actions follow positive thoughts. This should not come as a surprise to anyone, as it is really just common sense. Max further stated that when great strength or any great achievement comes about against all odds, through sheer determination and persistent hard work, it is more likely to last longer than when things come easy, to perhaps someone with great genetic gifts in the athletic arena. This is another example of the old adage of "easy-come, easy-go". In a book largely based on Maxick's training ideas, called "Philosophy, Science and Practice of Maxalding" there are a number of good pointers for practicing the art of visualization, though I'm not sure I agree 100 percent with the author on every one of them. I will list a few here that I do agree with and think are key concepts;

1. Concentrate in the flow of heat that the contraction of a muscle group produces and try to increase its effect mentally.

2. Tense your muscles very slowly feeling each part of the anatomy, each .fiber and direct all your thoughts to them. Relax very slowly too.

3. Try to imagine how each breath is contributing to replenish you of energy, how the oxygen flow is directed towards the contracted muscle.

4. Try to feel and imagine how your relaxed muscles grow during rest. Always go to bed with the firm belief that tomorrow you will be better and stronger.

5. Avoid boredom, it will be your worst enemy. Enjoy with each control and exercise. Try to excel yourself in every action.

I like these 5 ideas, but of course this is not a comprehensive list, and we will delve more into these concepts further on in the book.

One of the other concepts espoused by Maxick and his students is the idea that each man must develop his own individualized system which fits his idiosyncrasies and particular needs. While we may all start out in the physical culture game using someone else's set routine, eventually we must mature and grow and find our own way in the strength game if we are to truly maximize our efforts and the output and results thereof. It is a long process, really an unending one, comprised of one experiment after another with ourselves as the guinea pigs, discarding those things which do little for us and keeping and further refining those things which seem to work well. There really is no such thing as having "arrived" at the perfect program, as the body is never in a static state, but always in a dynamic, ever changing one. One must keep throwing the muscles new stimuli to keep them from growing stale, and of course the mind is the same way; boredom has derailed more promising training programs than physical injury or other factors, I would guess. **Court Saldo**, in his Maxalding brochure, said that "each person must be a law unto him or herself" and that no one fixed system could bring about guaranteed results in a cut & dried fashion for every student or trainee. Anyone who has been well read via muscle magazines, books or the internet knows just how potentially confusing things can be, especially for the novice, who comes across all kinds of seemingly contradictory information from a myriad of so-called reliable sources.

Author's Note*

Court Saldo was Monte Saldo's son, and taught the Maxalding course for many years after the passing of Monte and Max.

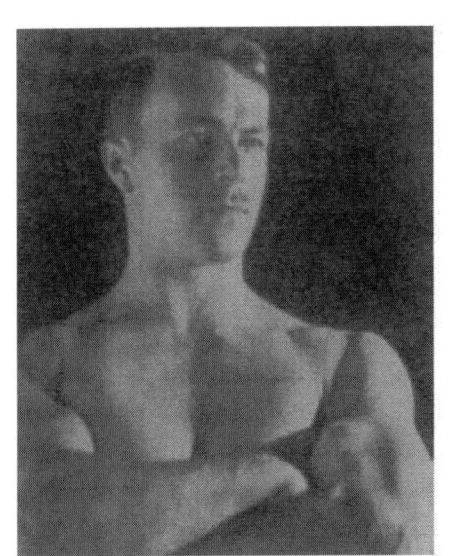

Figure 2. Court Saldo, youngest Monte's son, teached Maxalding until 1980 and perfected the system to its present form.

What works well for one person could actually be harmful to another, let alone ineffective. Franco Columbu said something that sounds very simplistic but is really far more profound than it sounds; basically he said that if something works for you, it works, regardless of what anyone says about it or what the so-called science behind it or lack thereof is. This is a good idea to bear in mind in your development of your personalized system. Maxick said that anything that we do that is accompanied by much thought is bound to have far more profound and long lasting effects than things which come to us passively. Like other great trainers of his era, Maxick strongly suggested the positive ideas of getting pleasurable exercise on a regular basis as part of one's regular "routine". Things like walking the dog, gardening, fishing, kayaking, etc, are all valid forms of relaxing exercise, though you seldom hear such things suggested as having any value in the typical power or Olympic lifter's training protocol. Maxick wrote about the results of his unique form of Muscle Control, with its visualization and mental imagery components leading to an eventual symphony between the brain and the body, starting with a notable clarity of mind and then an increased responsiveness of the body to the control of the mind. He put a premium on the state of relaxation, not a lazy or lethargic state of mind, but on the contrary a state of heightened awareness without the associated anxiety levels.

There have been some great athletes who seem to have this quality, and they tend to standout from the crowd. They might seem almost disinterested because they appear to be so calm, but this is a false notion. Their concentration is focused to the max. It just doesn't look that way. Maxick, again like others in his day, suggested that we not worry as it robs our energy and causes poor health. Truth be told, this is even a biblical principle written about by David in the Psalms and reiterated elsewhere throughout the scriptures.

Jesus spoke these words in Matthew Chapter 6:

Matthew 6:25

For this reason I say to you, [fn]do not be worried about your [fn]life, *as to* what you will eat or what you will drink; nor for your body, *as to* what you will put on. Is not life more than food, and the body more than clothing?

	Mat 6:26	"Look at the birds of the [fn]air, that they do not sow, nor reap nor gather into barns, and *yet* your heavenly Father feeds them. Are you not worth much more than they?
	Mat 6:27	"And who of you by being worried can add a *single* [fn]hour to his [fn]life?
	Mat 6:28	"And why are you worried about clothing? Observe how the lilies of the field grow; they do not toil nor do they spin,
	Mat 6:29	yet I say to you that not even Solomon in all his glory clothed himself like one of these.
	Mat 6:30	"But if God so clothes the grass of the field, which is *alive* today and tomorrow is thrown into the

|Mat 6:31

> furnace, *will He* not much more *clothe* you? You of little faith!
>
> "Do not worry then, saying, 'What will we eat?' or 'What will we drink?' or 'What will we wear for clothing?'

You get the idea. I must say that I don't fully agree with everything that Maxick said. He said something about a completely free mind being in absolute control connects one to the infinite. This sounds a lot like Eastern Religious philosophies espoused by some advanced practitioners of Yoga, transcendental Meditation and the like, with which I strongly differ. I believe very strongly that the only thing that truly connects one to the infinite in the correct way is a personal relationship with Jesus Christ, but I will not get on a soap box here and expound any further on this, just making my thoughts clear in this area. I will conclude this section about Maxick here, but you might see his name pop up again here and there throughout this book.

More on the topic from Bradley Steiner:

Mental power, concentration, goal-oriented visualization of your training aims, or whatever you want to call it, is the single most important factor for success in lifting. **I have known persons to overcome every type of handicap – physical and psychological – through the use of their iron will and their resolute determination to succeed in attaining their goal. The Mind is what does it!** *Truly, the greatest obstacle to the attainment of achievement as a lifter lies within your mind. Gravity is overcome by persistent physical training, but the task of doing the training, in good times and bad, remains a mental problem; and it can be satisfactorily overcome only through the proper employment of your mind power.*

We can easily compare the mind to the role of the General or Commander in Chief of an army, with the physical body being the army itself. The body, just as in the case of an actual military force, functions efficiently only in direct **proportion to the efficiency of the commands issued forth by the General. If that General lacks** *ability in directing his army, then the troops, no matter their potential excellence, cannot achieve the objective. So too with the mind and the body.*

Here is more from Bradley;

Bradley Steiner Persistence: A Must for Progress by Bradley J. Steiner (1975) Success, as somebody once aptly put it, is the result of 1% inspiration and 99% perspiration. This applies no matter what the particular field may be, but it is more literally applicable to physical training than it is to almost anything else. Unless you're really willing to sweat, you're unlikely to achieve much success in barbell work. Great lifters or physique men are made, not born - they are self-made via their own diligent, grueling efforts. One of the most self-defeating - and common - things that many trainees in the iron game do is play what I call the stop-start training game, or the this-routine, that-routine training game. Perhaps you're familiar with them yourself. In the stop-start training game the lifter spends about six hours mapping out the schedule that will turn him into the next great champion. Or perhaps he decides to follow a time-honored system such as Peary Rader's Master Bodybuilding Course. No matter; our hero somehow gets set with something he has reason to believe is an excellent course or program. And he works out diligently -- for a week or two. Then something happens. After realizing that even the best training system on earth requires work if it is to be productive, the trainee experiences his first discouragement. Those exercises that were so invigorating and challenging during the first couple of workouts have now become an almost ominous task. It's hard work to force yourself to grind out those heavy exercises! Magic has no place in lifting. We get what we pay for. So after rationalizing to himself, the trainee skips "just one" -- or maybe two -- workouts. Then reluctantly, he tries to resume his training. Since he's already discouraged himself, the oomph isn't there, and he is forced to reduce his poundages. He pushes himself a bit and manages to train steadily for three weeks before stopping again. "Man, this is hard work." After a layoff of maybe five or six days the trainee goes back to the weights.

He trains for another few weeks, stops, then starts again, and so on, ad nauseum. Well, no wonder he's unlikely to attain any sufficient gains in strength and development. He lacks persistance. The this-routine, that-routine game is also great sport among many who call themselves barbell men. It works this way: A trainee reads about a great routine in a new article. The schedule, the article says, in no uncertain terms will turn him into a veritable mountain of rippling muscle and strength. So he tries the routine. Next month he not only realizes that he is no mountain, but also that he is, alas, the same rotten mole hill, and he feels disgusted. The same magazine, however, has a new and even better system next month that makes every other method shamefully obsolete -- including last month's. So the trainee, always reluctant to exercise a little persistance on a single course of action, plunges headfirst into a new routine. He tries this latest "wonder method" for a month -- until he sees another routine that's "even better" and switches again . . . and so it goes, on and on and on. Now, be honest with yourself. Which, if not both, of these games are you guilty of playing? Stop kidding yourself, friendo. You will never get anywhere with either of them. Copping out doesn't build muscles. Persistence is as necessary as hard work for good results in bodybuilding or lifting. Sporadic efforts are valueless because the body requires steady demands if it is to make steady progress. It's a simple equation. And that is why, admittedly, very, very few men will succeed in reaching their ultimate goals. Very few people will force themselves -- and I mean force themselves -- to exercise the simple willpower that is required to continue on. They like to believe that there's some easier, less demanding way. Unfortunately, there isn't. Steady, grueling, untiring efforts -- even on only a few basic exercises -- are what ultimately produce outstanding results. Bill Pearl didn't develop his body by changing schedules whenever the whim struck him. Neither did John Grimek, Casey Viator, Reg Park or Sergio Oliva. No man on earth ever developed a tremendously muscular and powerful body without sticking to his training. It's that simple. The exercises that are producing the greats of today are the same exercises that produced the greats of yesteryear. It is not so much what schedule of exercises you follow that affects whether you gain satisfactorily or not, but rather how hard and how persistently you follow whatever effective routine you like. Of course, it's not easy to stay on a tough program of exercises week after week while continuously pushing yourself to work harder and still harder, but who ever said that it is supposed to be easy to accomplish anything worthwhile in life? After the initial period of enthusiasm for a workout schedule wains, the fun really starts. It's up to you to grit your teeth and actually force yourself to keep at it. I think that it's about time this simple fact was emphasized. There is no magic in this world or in life. The trainee who understands this and who knows that it's up to him to keep working to achieve and maintain his physical excellence is miles ahead of everyone else. Understand that success means steady effort and you've jumped the first five hurdles on your way to achieving your goals. Please understand that, so long as you're on an effective program, it is the effort you pour into what you do that makes it work. Here's a story that illustrates the importance of sticking to it. I once knew an intelligent but exceptionally unathletic young man. Let's call him Bob. Bob could never muster any enthusiasm for sports or athletics of any kind, and, frankly, being a naturally small-boned person, he looked as if he'd never spent even two hours a month doing anything more strenuous than walking. When Bob was 17, he became concerned about his rather underdeveloped body. Girls were as important to Bob as books, and to say the least, he wanted very much to build himself up so he could look and feel more manly. He wanted strength and physical confidence! Bob was quite determined to rectify his poor condition, and he asked me to put him on an exercise schedule. I did so, half expecting him to drop it midway of the first week of training. Boy, was I ever wrong. Bob purchased a moderately heavy -- 110 pound -- barbell set. He trained religiously on the routine I gave him and more than once in the initial months of training I openly told him that I admired his determination. As the months rolled by, Bob began buying additional plates to add to the poundages he was using. He added a squat rack and then a flat bench to his modest but effective home gym. I especially respected him because he was one of the slowest gainers I had ever met in my life. Yet slow progress didn't dampen his ardor for progress. He managed to go from 142 to 150 pounds in three months. Today, a year and a half after his first workout, Bob weighs 176, and it's solid muscle.

He has trained three times a week for about an hour each session and has only taken two one-week layoffs during the course of his brief but strenuous career with the weights. His workouts take only about 90 minutes, ad he has successfully combined them with his school work and his dating. Does Bob enjoy training? Actually, no, he doesn't. But being a sensible, logical fellow, he feels that four or five hours a week spent at a difficult task is worthwhile -- if it enhances every other second of his life. And he feels and looks so good today that he's starting to like his training. Nevertheless, regardless of how he happens to feel, Bob trains. Bob has followed only two different programs during his training career. They are as follow: PROGRAM ONE Presses Curls Bench Presses Power Cleans Squats Leg Raises PROGRAM TWO Behind the Neck Presses Bent-over Rows Bench Presses Curls Stiff Legged Deadlifts Sit-ups Squats. Bob is one example of success gained by persistent effort. Of course, everyone is different, and your own aspirations may go higher than Bob's. That is all the more reason why you'll need persistence to achieve your chosen goals. One of the greatest things weight training can do for a man is teach him to be disciplined and to be patient. He must discipline himself to perform the rigors of his scheduled workouts, and he must be patient enough to keep working out until he begins to see the results of those workouts. And those results will be more than enough reason to keep at it.

Some words on Muscle control by Harry Paschall:

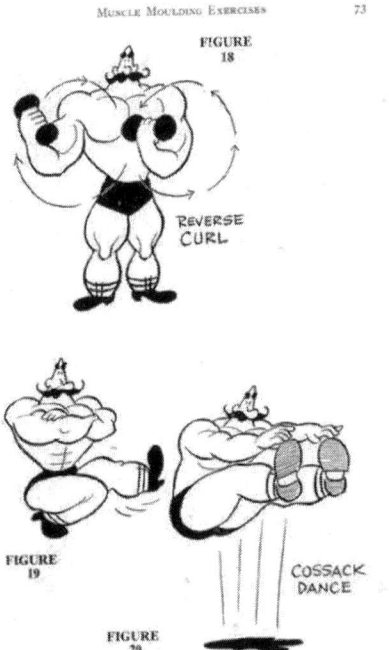

Here is one of Harry's famous BOSCO cartoons

In shaping the muscles, we must not overlook the value of muscle control. The greats of the game have been men who devoted a lot of time to mental massage of the muscle groups. Sandow, Grimek, Klein, Park, and all the other outstanding stars have learned to flex, flick and ripple every muscle band in the arm simply by thinking about it. This mental control has a very beneficial effect on the very shape of the muscles. The biceps themselves learn to leap higher at the word of command. It is well to rest the arms between exercises by flexing them, waving them loosely, making the muscles ebb and flow, ebb and flow, ebb and flow. You can also add to the effectiveness of certain "cramp" movements by exerting this mental control to fully flex the muscle while using a weight. Old-timers like Max Sick and Otto Arco carried this mental control to such peaks of efficiency that their arms were tremendous when measured in the flexed position. Arco had 17-in. biceps when weighing about 140 lb. A point worth remembering, however, is that these short men had superlative all-round development, without a single weak link in the chain. They were just as strong as they looked.

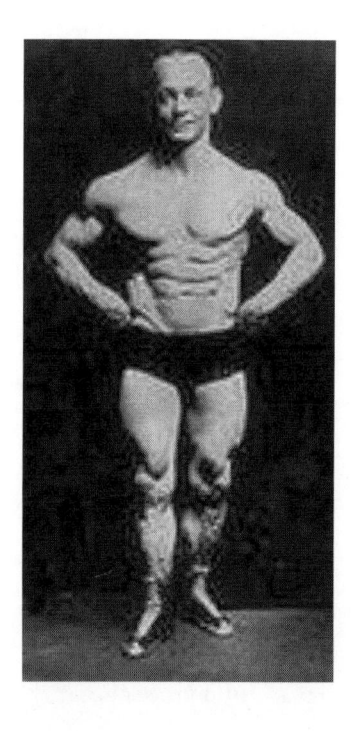

Otto Arco

What is the difference between a successful trainee and a not so successful one?

What is it that a handful of guys in the gym possess that seems to set them apart from "the crowd"? Many in "the crowd" would write it off as the juice, or say something like "that guy is a freak of nature", speaking of the person's God- given genetics. While either of the above or even both of the above could indeed be true, there really is more to it than that. While having been blessed with good genes goes a long way in helping folks reach a high level in many sports and athletic and strength related endeavors, and anabolic enhancement can potentially get one to that level a bit faster, **neither of these is an absolute requirement for greatness.** Many people that have tremendous physical or mental gifts never make the best use of them, and a good many don't use them at all. Most if not all of the people that point out the success of others as being tied to genetics have not even scratched the surface of their own genetic potential. I would venture to say that none of us really has any idea of just how much potential we possess, and further, that *few of us ever come remotely close to realizing that potential.* Steroids can and do indeed help folks get bigger, faster, and stronger more quickly than non-enhanced athletes, but there is no "free lunch". The benefits come with the very real potential for some very ugly negative side effects. Some folks are inclined to minimize the dangers of steroids and adopt the mental attitude of "damn the torpedoes, full speed ahead". Those of us who consider ourselves as "hard gainers" or whom are looking for short cuts will be tempted by the lure of so-called easy gains associated with anabolic agents. As a former user myself, let me dispel the myth that steroids preclude the need for hard work; they do not. I would also ask you to take a long, hard look at the longevity records of those who have used steroids to boost their careers. You may find some rare exceptions, but generally, steroids will get one farther faster, but will not keep one there for the long haul, and may in fact be a real factor in the cutting short of many a promising athlete's career in the long term.

One of the reasons I gave up "the juice" many years ago was because I'm in it for the long haul. While many of my peers at that time were seeking to reach some goal as quickly as possible and then sit back and rest on the laurels of that achievement, I truly enjoyed working out for the sheer joy of it, not just for the rewards of winning competitions and trophies. **Joy in working out? What was that I said??** Yes, absolutely and unequivocally JOY, that's right. If you find no pleasure in working out, but rather find it tedious, boring, or a chore, I am afraid you are destined to be just "one of the crowd", an also-ran; one of those denizens of the gym that spends lots of time there, but seldom if ever shows any real sign of progress. You know who it is that I refer to, don't you? **Arnold Schwarzenegger** spoke of working out with *ferocity and joy*, which initially may strike you as an oxymoron; do these two words belong together in any format? **I understand what he was talking about and have experienced it myself.** Why *ferocity,* you ask? When you start your training period, regardless of the exact methodology you choose, you must be **the dominant buck, the alpha wolf or the soldier bee. There is no place for drones or spikes here.** You must have laser-like focus and intensity in order to succeed. You must approach the weights (in my case); chin up bar, tackling dummy, whatever tool you happen to be working with; as your *opponent*.

Arnold

Imagine yourself in exaggerated terms.

This may sound kind of silly at first, but trust me; there is nothing silly about it. There have been proponents of the idea of working out in a blind rage. Rage is associated with adrenalin, and I do not question that this would be effective to a degree. Some of the more recent pre-workout supplements I have come across ads in magazines for even have rage in their names.

However, rage has negative connotations, and maintaining this state of mind for your entire workouts would be stressful and very draining of energy. The ferocity and intensity associated with rage are the desirable qualities that you wish to extract and use. At the same time, you must have a positive, joyful, exhilarated state of mind, which comes from the confidence that with every set of every exercise, you are propelling yourself ever forward towards your goals. You know that there is no force on this earth that can stop you from your relentless pursuit of those goals. There is joy in the determination that you are ready to do whatever it takes. You will not be just another gym rat, just another also- ran. There is joy in the realization that you are the master of your own destiny to a very large extent, and that when you do all the right things, good things can not keep themselves from happening.

You must *conceive, believe, and achieve*. Sound trite or corny? Forget that idea; there is nothing corny about it.

Conceive what you want to accomplish, and be specific and realistic about it. Set a relatively short term goal of a personal best in the arena of your choice. You can have a longer term goal like becoming a world class whatever, but keep that on the back-burner and concentrate on the shorter term goal for now.

Long term goals are reached by reaching shorter term goals on a regular and consistent basis.

Once you have conceived of your goal, you must ***believe in yourself*** and in the basic principle that good things come to those who are willing to work at them.

There is nothing mystical or magical about it.

Refer back to that opening paragraph from Mr. Draper;

The secret is that there IS NO SECRET!

Works hard, work smart, eat right and rest fully, and your **body will have no choice but to respond accordingly** and grow and get stronger daily. This is where the achieving then comes in. It will follow the first two like morning follows night or spring follows winter.

It has no choice but to do so.

The animal kingdom has many examples that we could point to as analogous in some ways to the human condition. I alluded to this concept above. The alpha male wolf, the dominant buck whitetail deer, and the "soldier" bee are but a few of the examples of what we would consider as "successful", relative to their animal counterparts. The big difference between the animal kingdom and us is that we have a great deal *more control* of our own destinies.

In the animal kingdom, genetics pretty much dictate which animals will be the dominant ones and accordingly, the most successful reproducers and feeders. We humans, on the other hand, can largely choose and determine our own destinies. It may well be true that many of our characteristics and traits are inherited from our parents and their parents and grandparents, and on down the line, it is also true that **will power, determination and "stick-to-itiveness" can overcome almost any perceived genetic flaw or weakness.** Going back to the animals, I read recently a quote about dogs that is really more fitting for and I think aimed at humans.

"It's not the size of the dog in the fight; it's the size of the fight in the dog"

Truer words have seldom been spoken, my friends! The men that achieve great feats of engineering or invent things that change the world are not always those that are blessed with a massive I.Q. Albert Einstein said that genius was 10% inspiration and 90% perspiration. The same ideas hold true in the physical realm; the strongest men are not always the biggest men, and the "toughest" men are not always the biggest or the strongest men. Some men by all appearances are fearless, but much more often if not always, they have simply met their fears head on, faced them and overcome them. Courage and bravery are thought to be traits that are possessed by the fearless, but this is a mistake.

Courage is not the absence of fear, but the willingness to forge ahead and to continue fighting on despite it's presence in our minds.

We can allow it to get a grip on our hearts and minds and render us helpless and paralyzed, or with the help of God, we can march through the valley of death while "fearing no evil". What is it about the under-dog that so endears us to him? Why does the world celebrate when he overcomes all the odds and manages to become a victor despite the odds? Perhaps it is because we feel a certain kismet with the under-dog ourselves. We have all had to face experiences or are currently facing experiences that seem insurmountable or impossible to overcome. We have dreams of performing great feats and of vanquishing our foes, yet **we usually allow our fears and misgivings to get the best of us.** Our dreams stay in that nether world of our REM sleep, or maybe sneak their way into the occasional daydream, but never quite make it to fruition.

When we watch movies like the "Cinderella Man" or "Rocky", we briefly imagine ourselves overcoming the odds and beating the unbeatable as these heroes do.

Without a doubt, this is a desirable, exhilarating feeling and may be why movies such as these are so popular. We are inspired, at least for a moment or at best perhaps a day or two, until we relinquish ourselves to the concept that these things only happen in the movies, not in our real lives. In reality, Rocky Balboa was/is a fictional character, but the "Cinderella Man" was based on a very real man and real events, as was the movie "Invincible" (about Vince Pappale getting on the Eagles team with no college or pro ball in his background). The movie "The 300" was also based on factual events, and I could name others.

Little guys like the Shepherd David have been slaying giants like Goliath all through history, and these things are still happening in our time, and we continue to write them off as "freak events" like lightning striking the same spot twice.

We attribute these events to "luck", or happenstance. We can continue to relegate our dreams to the nether world. We can continue on eking out a meager existence of mediocrity and averageness. We can, and will continue to seek excuses and find circumstances or other people to blame for our never reaching the heights we aspire to and dream of. Most of us will do just that, and will be haunted throughout our remaining time on this planet wondering "**what if**?" We will lament the could haves, should haves and would haves of our lives and try to content ourselves with our ever growing list of excuses, but this will never quite cut the mustard. We will be plagued by the knowledge that we did not give our all or our best efforts in life. We left something in the tank. We failed to go the extra mile or reach beyond ourselves. When the going got tough, we tossed in the towel. This is the perfect recipe for becoming a miserable old man or woman, of which the world is full, unfortunately.

How many gifted, talented, blessed people end up as bums, never even reaching the status of has-beens? They fit more into the category of a never was, which is far worse.

On the other hand, **you can determine** this very moment that you will not become that miserable old man or woman. You will not spend your "golden years" regretting all the things you might have done. So what does this decision really mean? What are the practical ramifications of such a decision? Well, we started on the premise that you are a fitness trainee of some genre, and not that you are trying to become the president of the United States or the richest man in the world. (Let's keep first things first, after all.)

If you seek to become the best lifter, the best bodybuilder, the best football player, etc. that you are capable of being, then;

Every workout or training event will be seen as a mission.

That does not mean that every lifting session will be a max effort one or every running session will be done at top speed or for maximum distance. Different training sessions will be aimed at training different aspects of the things needed to reach the overall goal. For example, powerlifting is not as simple as it is often thought to be by outsiders to the sport. Raw strength, speed of movement and technique all play important roles in powerlifting. Accordingly, some training sessions will be aimed at improving technique, others will be about speed and explosiveness, and still others aimed at raw brute strength improvement. **You must be fully focused on the task at hand**, and not the one you will be working on tomorrow or the next day, or during the next week.

This is where **having a plan comes in**. Intensity does no good if it has no intentional and well designed focus.

This is why sports teams have coaches, and why it's not a bad idea for rookie trainees to work with a good personal trainer or coach, at least for some period of time. At an absolute minimum, one must pick or custom design a routine to train on, which provides some direction as to what body parts, what exercise or what skills will be addressed at which times and in what type of order and frequency. Just as important as the training is, proper nutrition and recuperation are also required to make the most of the hard work you put in on the field or in the gym. You will read and hear about individuals that live on big Macs and soda, or some other ridiculous thing as their post workout nutrition regimen, and they make gains just the same. Powerlifters in the larger weight classes have somewhat of a reputation for ingesting all manner of poor quality calories. They never met a calorie they didn't like, regardless of its nature or origin. Consuming massive quantities of food in order to pack on mass will get one stronger, if for no other reason than the improvement in leverage that occurs. It is also easier to gain muscle and fat together instead of trying to gain pure muscle without the fat. Though it may be easier to pack on the mass that way, it is not very healthy, especially in the long term. A larger waist line has been clearly correlated with increased risk for heart problems, high blood pressure, etc. You will read or hear about trainees that get 3 or 4 hours of sleep a night and that love to drink and party all night long after a hard workout. They somehow manage to make gains. Let me assure you of a couple of things along these lines; First of all, they would be making even better gains if they did the proper things outside of the gym or off of the playing field. Secondly, this lifestyle will very likely catch up with them eventually with very negative effects. Make no mistake; you will reap just what you sow. You have surely heard the expression "burning the candle at both ends". It makes no sense. I did a bit of that myself as a younger man, I must admit. Young men with surging hormones often think of themselves as indestructible and think that eating poorly and ingesting toxins like drugs and excessive alcohol will have no ill effects. They indulge in silly contests of machismo, trying to out-poison each other and yet survive. This type of thing is even endeared to us in popular culture and literature.

James Bond sucks down a few dry martinis before vanquishing the bad guys. Conan the barbarian spends a night in a pub, pouring down ale or Meade before engaging in mortal combat.

Conan

We buy into this stuff and try to emulate it. While the negative effects may not surface immediately or profoundly, sooner or later they will. It is often assumed that because gains are being made, the negative effects of one's lifestyle are negligible or non-existent. The reality is that gains would be greatly improved with a better diet and moderation of recreational substances. I am not getting on a soap box and railing against having a beer or a glass of wine or whatever libation you may prefer. I am just suggesting that these things are often way over done, only to our own undoing. Some of the greatest athletes in the world have fallen victim to the ravages of drugs and alcohol abuse with often very tragic consequences. "All things in moderation" is a good thought along these lines.

Many of today's broken down ex athletes that are plagued with arthritis, cardiopulmonary disease, high blood pressure, blood sugar problems, etc., were those who chose earlier in life to disregard the sound principles of proper nutrition and rest/recuperation. Now I'll grant you, a lot of these issues are genetically related, but while you may have a genetic predisposition to one of these conditions, you can greatly improve your chances by "clean living". In researching for my books, *"**Forgotten Secrets of the Old Time Strongmen**"*, and *"**The Secrets of Age Defying Strength, and how to obtain it"**,* I read many an old training course and biography of the strongest men of the last two centuries. I searched for commonalities between them. The men who had the highest longevity as well as great and enduring strength had a couple of things in common, for the most part. One of the things they had in common was that they did some form of cardio type or more general conditioning training and **not just strength training.** Another thing in common was moderation of stimulants, depressants and other potentially toxic substances, and the **emphasis on good, sound nutrition.** Even back then, wise men of strength refrained from excessive intakes of red meat and sugar, and sought out a good variety of vegetables, fruits, nuts and other more **organic foods as staples** in their daily diets. One thing to keep in mind is that in those times, produce probably contained more nutrition, and both produce and dairy and meat contained more nutrition and less harmful substances like artificial hormones. There were less pre-packaged foods, convenience foods and highly refined foods than are prevalent in our modern diets. Another thing worth mentioning is that a lot of those old time strength greats **were not huge men**, even by the standards of that era. **Eugene Sandow, the Mighty Atom, George Hackenschmidt, Milo Steinborn** and others were small by the standards of the current batch of strongmen like you might see winning bodybuilding contests at top levels or competing on "The World's Strongest Man" events. The other thing in common for all of these men was **attitude**. They all wrote about and strongly emphasized the proper attitude being of utmost importance in their ultimate success.

Sandow said that doing one set with the proper attitude, focus and intensity was worth at least 10 sets of "going through the motions"

Sandow

The Mighty Atom

The Mighty Atom was a midget compared to many of today's strength greats, yet he pulled airplanes with his hair and bit nails into pieces, *largely by using his tremendous mental focusing abilities, which he went to great lengths developing.* Muscles are controlled by nerves, and nerves are controlled by the brain. Some muscular contractions go on at a sub-conscious level, while others are contracted by "voluntary" control. There are those who would tell you that at some level, even some of the so-called involuntary contractions can be consciously controlled by those who are more in tune with their own bodies. Yogis claim to be able to do this at least to some extent. *That is practitioners of Yoga, not Yogi bear!* There is no doubt that there is a strong link between the mind, the CNS and muscle action. Visualization, self hypnosis and other methods along these lines have been and continue to be used to enhance strength and motor skills.

Setting a new personal record by doing more weight or adding a repetition requires a positive attitude and mindset.

You must first imagine yourself doing it, visualize or "see" yourself actually making the lift over and over in your mind, and your body/ mind will be *pre programmed for success*. If you were to scan through some of the more recent hard core muscle magazines being published these days, you would find many advertisements for supplements which mention the mind somehow. Words like "*pschychotropic*" or "*pschychoactive*" come up quite often. Names like "Dark Rage" are used for some of these new supplements. Ingredients that increase focus, aggression, alertness are now commonly found in pre-workout supplements. This comes as no surprise to me, as I understand that the industry is trying to reproduce steroid like results with natural or at least, hopefully, legal substances. One of the "benefits" of anabolic steroid usage is *increased aggressiveness*, which is a two edged sword. While increased aggressiveness in the gym can be a good thing to a certain extent, it can be dangerous in polite society.

It is one thing to consider a barbell or some other inanimate object as your opponent, perhaps even your enemy and *"attack"* it as such during an actual lift. Flying around the gym in a blind rage for the entirety of a workout is all together different, and really not the way to go. Just the term "blind rage" denotes a certain **lack of focus**, which is never a good thing when in the process of performing a potentially life threatening maximum weight single repetition lift attempt. You certainly want to be alert and wide awake during such an undertaking, thus a certain amount of a mild stimulant, such as caffeine might be acceptable for pre-workout ingestion. Keep in mind that this can be and often is over done. There is definitely such a thing as **over-stimulation** which can result in the jitters, loss of focus, even paranoia in severe cases. Adrenalin will do a pretty good job of getting you "jacked" all by itself when you are getting ready to perform a maximum lift attempt, and for many, no more external stimulation is needed.

Some experimentation may be required to discover just the proper stimulation level for you.

Another factor in this equation is the length of time you will need to stay in a heightened state of alertness or readiness to do battle. This is one of the biggest challenges a powerlifter will face in 3 lift competition, especially when there are lots of fellow competitors needing to complete warm-ups and 3 attempts at each of the 3 lifts over the course of the day. If you get all "jacked up" to perform your squats, it will be difficult to be that excited again by the time you attempt your final deadlift. It is good to be in a relaxed state in between heavy attempts, especially in the event that this becomes an extended period of time. This is a big reason you may wish to avoid stimulants or at the very least large doses of them at a meet, especially in the early phases. You may want to save it for later in the meet, when you might otherwise start running out of gas. Many top level athletes are currently practicing some form of visualization, or even self-hypnosis as a regular part of their training program. This can take various forms.

Generally, just filling one's mind with **positive thoughts about training and competing** is the key, and there are lots of ways used to go about this.

Athletes tend to put themselves, or allow others to put them under undue stress. Phrases like "***I must win***", "***I have to make this next lift***", or things along these lines put pressure on the trainee or competitor and **do not really help in achieving the best result.**

Associating pleasure and a sense of well being with a competitive or difficult training event has a much more beneficial result.

A competition should be a pleasant and enjoyable experience in order to be a successful one. That does not mean it won't require lots of effort or that it will be "easy". Thoughts along the lines of;

"***I am thrilled and honored to be involved in this event***", "***I am doing what I love to do today***", or "***I will have the best performance ever today***"

These are the kinds of positive reinforcing thoughts that should be prevalent. When negative thoughts try to sneak in (and rest assured they will), they must be pushed out with a replacement positive thought. Feed yourself a steady mental diet of positive thoughts and ideas constantly, both while training and while resting in between sets or in between training events, and you develop a mindset that leads to being the best you can be in competition as well.

A mind filled with happy, positive, reassuring thoughts leaves no room for damaging negative thoughts.

Some folks may think that this is narcissistic or is some type of an ego trip or something like that, but it really is not. There is a big difference between positive self reinforcement thinking and being on an ego trip, though sometimes the difference is not so obvious. We may even feel a bit guilty in telling ourselves "I will set a personal record today", or "I will win today". We may even have some misgivings about this kind of thinking that come from our religious or faith background. Clearly, if you acknowledge God as I do, there will be an implied prerequisite thought to any and all others that will go along the lines of "God willing".... I will do x, y or z.

My thinking in this realm is that God desires us to put forth our best efforts in all we do, and that while we must certainly acknowledge Him and his will in everything we do, dwelling on positive reinforcement concepts does not go against the idea that God is ultimately in charge. As long as our thoughts are not obviously miss- aligned with what we know to be God's will or we become so self absorbed in our training that we neglect our all important communion with God or with our family and friends, I don't think that the ideas I'm talking about here run counter to what God desires of us. There is a school of thought in which the *self* is all important; that we can reach our own level of deity somehow at the proper level of self awareness or self realization. I am not a student or a teacher of that kind of thinking, let me assure you. The mind is surely a powerful thing, but the best that can be manifested of it comes when it is subjected to the much more powerful and higher authority of its creator, in my opinion.

Visualization training techniques

There are differing kinds of visualization training, at least as I see it. On the one hand there is the type that starts outside of the training area and takes place when the mind is in a state of relaxation.

This type involves sitting or reclining in a comfortable position, breathing slowly and deeply, and inducing a state of extreme calm and relaxation, yet full awareness.

Once the proper relaxation level is obtained, the mind is prepared to accept positive thoughts and suggestions. Going even deeper than simply feeding oneself positive thoughts, one can actually visualize going through an actual workout or even a competition. If the proper state of mind is reached, one can smell, hear, taste and see all of the smells, sounds, tastes and visions that would normally be encountered during such an event.

The practitioner sees himself doing everything from getting dressed and doing warm-ups to performing his maximum effort event successfully.

If you cannot imagine or literally visualize yourself doing something, it is unlikely that you will be able to bring about the reality of it.

If you see and have seen yourself doing a thing over and over in your mind, the body will simply follow through and perform as it has been programmed to perform.

Of course, the physical training is part (a big part) of the equation and is not to be overlooked. But even with all the proper training under one's belt, the maximum effort event will not be successful without the proper attitude and mind set. Setting aside a short period a couple of times per week to do this visualization technique may pay off in a big way. You can do a short visualization technique almost anytime that you have a few minutes of free time, and it can't hurt.

Visualization works much like and may even be considered as a form of self hypnosis.

Hypnosis has been used to help folks lose weight, quit smoking and other bad habits and has done many other good things, although some would say it had no effect on them.

\If the person being hypnotized does not have a compliant attitude towards it or writes off hypnotism as bogus, it will be of little or no value.

Hypnosis and visualization both begin with relaxation as the starting point. Relaxation helps to un- clutter the mind and clear it of the many distractions that might otherwise occur. When the mind is in this tranquil, mellow and calm state, it is primed to accept the suggestions and thoughts that you wish to feed it. As you might imagine, there can be a negative side to this, if one were to allow themselves to be hypnotized by someone with other than the best intentions.

Most if not all proponents of these methods would tell you that you can not be hypnotized into doing something that you would never do normally because of moral or ethical objections, however.

Of course, with self hypnosis or self visualization, **you are in control** of the suggestions and thoughts that will be fed to the mind. It is suggested to do this in an environment that is soothing, stress free and which promotes relaxation. Another method of visualization is a more casual and fun approach, at least in my opinion.

In this form, the trainee simply begins visualization at the start of a physical training session.

This can be an unscripted, more "spur of the moment" type of thing, and can even vary as you would like it to from one training session to the next. It can be specifically tailored to training a certain body part if so desired.

As an example, one might visualize/imagine their arms expanding to the point where they are busting out of the sleeves during a bicep training episode.

Imagine your entire body expanding and breaking buttons, etc, like the incredible hulk when he gets angered. If you are a runner, you might think of yourself as having jetpacks on your back, propelling you forward at an unprecedented pace. (Think Roadrunner cartoon, for example)You might also take a more generalized approach, and take on the persona of a favorite movie or book hero, or if that seems corny to you, just think of yourself as a different version of yourself; one that is completely focused on the task at hand, and which can not be swayed or side-tracked from performing every set as if it was the most pressing thing in the world at that moment. (No pun intended, sorry)

You can have a *"**trigger**"* for transforming into this mode, and it will become like turning on a switch before you start your training.

This trigger should be one that you come up with and are comfortable with, and it could be something as simple as turning your cap backwards, or passing a certain threshold in your home, etc. Part of your "outside the gym" visualizing experience can consist of visualizing the details involved with your trigger and how it works, when it works, etc. You can use visual "cues" or other sensory "cues". If you tune more senses to trigger, you will be in better shape. The more fully lifelike and realistic your visualizations are, with every sensory perception tuned in, the more likely you will be to carry out **the performance that is practiced during the visualization.**

Practice makes perfect

We have all heard this statement before, perhaps to the point where it has simply become trite and even annoying to a degree. Nevertheless, it holds true in many areas of life, including strength and fitness training.

Visualization is an awesome way of adding practice sessions of your desired training protocol without actually draining your physical capacities while doing it.

When you do your visualization sessions, you will be able to execute perfect form on every rep of every set, which will translate ultimately into physically training that way, too.

A "memory" that is implanted in your mind through visualization is every bit as "real" as the memory of an actual experience.

Your mind will not be able to distinguish between the two once you have become well versed in the technique.

Remember the mind/nerve/muscle connection.

The muscles are controlled by the nerves which are attached to them. The nerves are controlled by the brain, connected at the other end.

It is not a democracy; the mind is an absolute dictator!

Visual Cues

One visual cue that can be used is commonly found in home gyms and commercial gyms all over the world. Posters and pictures of bodybuilding, strength and athletic heroes have been inspiring trainees for a long time. The properly "tuned in" individual can take these cues to a level beyond what is the norm, however. It is one thing to look at one of these posters or photos with admiration and think to oneself "I wish I could look like that" (read: lift like that, run like that, etc.) To take it to the next level, the viewer must **put himself in the picture.**

He must become the hero in the picture and perform as such.

Feel your every sinew bristling with raw energy and brute, raw power. See and feel yourself hoisting that massive weight off the floor. See yourself in the future, as the person you wish to be in that future, but see that person as **you, right here and right now.** My wife loves to bust my chops over the fact that I have reprinted "Conan the Barbarian" book covers plastered on my home gyms walls, along with the standard workout charts for my various pieces of equipment and pictures of guys performing big lifts, etc. She is of the obviously invalid opinion that this is juvenile. I was an avid reader of Conan books as a young man, and most of us are familiar with Arnold's big screen renditions of the comic book and novel hero. The book covers depict an extremely muscled, usually angry looking and barbaric gentleman wielding some treacherous weaponry while being attacked by a pack of wolves or otherwise engaged in some harrowing situation that would render most of us mortals a quivering sack of spineless jelly. (You have seen the picture above) Sometimes when I am preparing for a monumental set or a max single lift effort, I peer into one of these pictures, imagining what is going through Conan's mind as he is engaged in some life threatening battle, yet again.

There is no place for fear or doubt here.

I feel myself summoning the mindset of Conan in that situation. It is a mindset of utter, total and complete focus on the adversary to be vanquished. Conan is not thinking about his next mortgage payment or what he will be having for dinner later on. I try to "become" Conan in a sense, just for the duration of that next set. I do not fear the weight; I do not have misgivings or second thoughts. There is nothing else in the world for those 30-60 seconds but the weight and me. I do not think "I'm going to try very hard to lift this weight now", but rather, simply, "I will lift this weight now".

Any doubt that creeps into your mind must be *"**displaced**"* rather than dismissed. You **must consciously replace the negative thought with a corresponding positive thought to take its place.**

Much like the idea you surely have come across before that states that an idle pair of hands are "the devil's workshop", a mind not filled with positive thoughts is one that invites and allows negative thoughts to barge in and overtake the mind.

The concept of CHI or KI

What can an athlete who is not a martial artist learn from martial artists? This may strike you as an odd question. What do the martial arts have to do with or have in common with lifting weights, playing football, running a race, etc? One of the **most sought after and a highly desired skill in the martial arts,** regardless of the particular genre or style, is the idea of **mastering one's "CHI" or "KI".** What is this, exactly? It is defined a bit differently by various writers on the subject and seekers of its powers. For some, it has certain "mystical" connotations, while for others it is more "scientific". In its most simplistic definition, it could perhaps be described as *"**focus**"*. I used to use a supplement years ago that was called "CHI power", which contained herbal stimulants which were supposed to **help you to focus more strongly.** It contained the herb **Ephedra**, among others, which ultimately was banned because people with hypertension and people who over used it had some complications and there were even some reported deaths. Frankly, I loved the stuff but used it sparingly and not too frequently as I was aware of the potential inherent dangers. I did feel more "focused" when under its influence. Actually, caffeine can offer a similar effect and is safer at suggested dosages. So, am I saying that you can achieve an optimal state of CHI simply by drinking a cup of coffee before engaging in your physical training? Ah, I wish it was that easy, but no, not exactly. On the other hand, for those who don't get over stimulated or have negative reactions to this CNS stimulant, it can be a step in the right direction.

Anything that increases your level of focus will help you to perform better in virtually any endeavor, be it of a mental or a physical nature.

There are a number of herbs which are reported to have positive effects in this regard and these are at least worthy of some experimentation, in my opinion. **Gingko Biloba** is one of these herbs. There are also non herbal supplements which are designed to enhance cognitive function, memory and focus to some degree, and some may indeed have some real value for athletes and those involved in physical training. Most of the writings about CHI that I have come across do not mention the chemically induced development or enhancement of CHI, but I still think it is something worthy of mentioning here. Some writers describe CHI as *"inner strength"* which must be developed in differing ways from conventional or "external strength", yet external strength is required to develop this internal strength fully. They write and say that CHI is the internal force that controls the already developed external force and **directs it and intensifies it.** Martial artists usually, if not always, describe CHI as something that **dwells in and is summoned from the abdominal region**, which is thought of as **the power center of the body.** Perhaps this is why the "ideal" martial artist's physique is one that sports a 6 pack that is envied by the rest of us. (A pose from Bruce Lee used to advertise his movie "**Enter the Dragon**" might spring to your mind here)

Deep breathing techniques are common to Yoga practitioners, Martial Artists, and usually those who seek the ultimate development of the CHI. Any physical trainer worth his salt will tell you that training the "***core***" is a vital component of overall health and fitness. There is a strong connection between a strong core or abdominal region, and the ability to breathe deeply and optimally.

Deep breathing involves the abdominal cavity and the diaphragm and indeed every deep breath starts there.

Watch a baby breathe, and this is easily observed. Deep breathing is also a vital component of the relaxation techniques that set the stage for visualization or self hypnosis practice, so again we see a common thread in these various methods. It helps to clear the mind of "clutter" or simply distracting thoughts **that would detract from full focus on the task at hand.** CHI is often associated with "***meridians***" or ***channels of energy flow*** in our bodies. The concepts of acupuncture, acupressure and EFT or "***Meridian Tapping***" are based on this. CHI is thought by many to be **the ability to harness and direct this internal flow of energy and to make it subject to the conscious mind and not just dictated and controlled by the subconscious.** An example of a martial artist using this would be in the breaking of a brick with the hand; the entire energy flow is directed to the hand for the instant it makes contact with the brick. If we could cause all or the majority of our energy to be directed to the muscles involved in a particular effort such as in the performing of a I rep max lift, imagine the possibilities.

Perhaps the flow of energy described by those who practice acupuncture and similar methods is not anything spiritual, magical or mystical, but rather **a way of describing the nervous system's connection to the parts which it controls, the musculature in particular.**

There have been various fitness trainers which espouse something in the realm of what may be called "***nerve force***" or something similar. Those who practice "muscle control", Kin Shi Hai Do, "Dynamic Tension" or "Virtual Resistance Training" might be familiar with the concept of "nerve force". This involves learning to better control the direction of the muscular contractions and forces thereof by **controlling the mind and its control over the CNS.**

You have heard the term "***mind over matter***", to be sure. I think we have all heard the story of the slightly built woman who somehow musters the strength to pick up the corner of a car to free her trapped child from under it in a desperate situation. The "***fight or flight***" response is partially responsible, if not solely responsible for things like this. It is not likely that the woman involved in this story was well practiced in the discipline of developing her CHI as part of some martial arts or other training. What is going on in this situation? How is it possible for a physically untrained person or anyone for that matter, to perform such a feat when it is suddenly "required"? I think there are a couple of things going on, the first of which is chemical in nature; the **Adrenaline spike** which is part & parcel of the "fight or flight" response. Another component of this response is the ***loss of inhibition*** that goes along with it. What do I mean by this? Normally, our brain inhibits our muscles from performing at their full capacity **to prevent us from hurting ourselves by over exertion.** The unbridled contraction of the muscles with no accompanied "braking" by opposing muscles could cause tendon, ligament or muscle damage and because this is true there are normally limits imposed by the brain and its subjugate, the CNS, to prevent such damage from occurring. In a life threatening situation such as the one posed by the child trapped beneath the car, the inhibitory responses are over ridden by the brain and the CNS, because when the body is engaged in an effort to preserve a life, the concern of tearing a muscle or tendon becomes trivial in comparison. I would be willing to wager that the woman in the story **suffered some torn muscles at the least and perhaps worse when she performed the feat in question.** I also suspect she was willing to deal with this consequence happily, as her actions also **saved the life of her child.**

Here is a brief but interesting story from the realm of science relating to the idea we are talking about here:

The Secret to Chimp Strength

Science Daily (Apr. 8, 2009) — February's brutal chimpanzee attack, during which a pet chimp inflicted devastating injuries on a Connecticut woman, was a stark reminder that chimps are much stronger than humans—as much as four-times stronger, some researchers believe. But what is it that makes our closest primate cousins so much stronger than we are? One possible explanation is that great apes simply have more powerful muscles. Indeed, biologists have uncovered differences in muscle architecture between chimpanzees and humans. But biologist Alan Walker, a professor at Penn State University, thinks muscles may only be part of the story. In an article published in the April issue of *Current Anthropology*, Walker argues that humans may lack the strength of chimps **because our nervous systems exert more control over our muscles.** Our fine motor control prevents great feats of strength, but allows us to perform delicate and uniquely human tasks. Walker's hypothesis stems partly from a finding by primatologist Ann MacLarnon.

MacLarnon showed that, relative to body mass, chimps have much less grey matter in their spinal cords than humans have.

Spinal grey matter contains large numbers of motor neurons—nerves cells that connect to muscle fibers and regulate muscle movement.

More grey matter in humans means more motor neurons, Walker proposes. And having more motor neurons means more muscle control. Our surplus motor neurons allow us to engage smaller portions of our muscles at any given time. We can engage just a few muscle fibers for delicate tasks like threading a needle, and progressively more for tasks that require more force. Conversely, since chimps have fewer motor neurons, each neuron triggers a higher number of muscle fibers. So using a muscle becomes more of an all-or-nothing proposition for chimps. As a result, chimps often end up using more muscle than they need. "And that is the reason apes seem so strong relative to humans," Walker writes. Our finely-tuned motor system makes a wide variety of human tasks possible. Without it we couldn't manipulate small objects, make complex tools or throw accurately. And because we can conserve energy by using muscle gradually, we have more physical endurance—making us great distance runners. Great apes, with their all-or-nothing muscle usage, are explosive sprinters, climbers and fighters, but not nearly as good at complex motor tasks. In other words, chimps make lousy guests in china shops. In addition to fine motor control, Walker suspects that humans also may have a neural limit to how much muscle we use at one time. Only under very rare circumstances are these limits bypassed—as in the anecdotal reports of people able to lift cars to free trapped crash victims. "Add to this the effect of severe electric shock, where people are often thrown violently by their own extreme muscle contraction, and it is clear that we do not contract all our muscle fibers at once," Walker writes. "So there might be a degree of cerebral inhibition in people that prevents them from damaging their muscular system that is not present, or not present to the same degree, in great apes." Walker says that testing his hypothesis that humans have more motor neurons would be fairly straightforward. However, he concedes that testing whether humans have increased muscle inhibition could be a bit more problematic.

What can we take away from this situation that might help us with our training demands, if anything? Is there a way for us to at least partially bypass our bodies natural inhibitory muscle shutdown or braking?

I think the answer to these questions is yes, to a degree at least. It would not be desirable to completely eliminate the response previously described, as this would open us up to serious injury potential. **It is desirable to reduce this response just enough to allow the muscles to go beyond what has previously been allowed.** It does not have to be a huge increment to make a considerable difference in our training. So how do we bring this about? I think the answer is a multi faceted one. I also think there are several (at least) pathways to go down that can help reach this goal. Another concept that is used by martial artists and related to the idea of CHI is the idea of visualizing punching or kicking ***through*** your target. In other words, if you are punching an opponent's nose, you are "aiming" for the back of his head, not just his nose. When you think hard about this idea, it becomes obvious that ***the same idea can be used in lifting, jumping, etc.*** You have heard the expression relating to many sports; "**follow through**". When you are bowling, for example, even after the ball has been released, you continue moving your arm and hand in the same direction it was headed before the release. The idea is that you don't "**put the brakes on**" too early and end up failing to complete the movement fully and properly. It can be a useful idea when it comes to weight training and other similar strength training movements.

Let's think about using this concept on **the bench press** for an example.

If you *visualize throwing the bar up towards the ceiling rather than simply pressing it to arms length, you are on the right track*.

This is a mental "**trick**" designed to enhance explosiveness and "**compensatory acceleration**". **Dr. Fred Hatfield** spoke about the concept of compensatory acceleration years before speed training became all the rage a la the Russians and Westside Barbell. It sounds complicated but it is really pretty simple.

Use speed to compensate for the normal "sticking point" that slows the bar down and ultimately stops its progress in the ROM. Explosive training, trying to generate as much acceleration of the bar as possible at the start of and throughout a lift is huge part of the power generation equation, and can not be overlooked.

Of course, in order to develop explosiveness and acceleration, sub maximal weights must be used, typically in the 50-75 percent of 1rm range. **Plyometrics** is another way of training for explosiveness, but this method goes beyond simple acceleration and speed, though these are vital components. Plyometrics also entails a stretch reflex response to generate more power. To simplify this idea;

When a muscle is stretched in the eccentric phase slightly, immediately before an ensuing contraction, the contraction will be a stronger and more forceful one.

Generating acceleration and speed immediately following the stretch phase is the other major component of the Plyometrics equation. Now I will grant you that many with physiology degrees and alphabet soup after their names would say the above statements are gross over-simplifications, but I am a firm follower of and believer in the KISS principle. Keep things as simple as possible. So, in the bench pressing example spoken of above; if we were actually throwing the bar, or perhaps more practically, a medicine ball off of our chest, and trying to throw it as high and with as much speed as we could muster, we would be practicing Plyometrics. If, on the other hand, we kept a grip on the bar throughout the set, but still tried to move it as explosively and quickly as possible for every repetition, we would simply be doing "speed work", also known as "dynamic effort" work, also known as simply **training explosively.**

Now, keep that second example in mind, where we are holding onto the bar throughout the set, but visualize throwing it through the roof on each rep, or at least visualize generating enough speed and force to do so but still holding onto the bar. This is where the concept of CHI used by the martial artists in punching THROUGH the target comes into play.

This is a way of "tricking" the bodies normal inhibitory response to put the brakes on in the last part of a repetition's ROM. Visualizing pushing, punching, kicking or throwing ***past*** the desired target **is a way of bypassing the subconscious braking that otherwise would inevitably happen.** When this type of training is practiced often enough, even with sub maximal weights, the explosiveness should carry over to a 1 rep max effort and you will have learned to generate enough compensatory acceleration to blow right through a previous sticking point, regardless of where that point is relative to the ROM. This is similar to the martial artist eventually breaking through a brick or thick piece of wood after having practiced with something easier to break, but using the technique of trying to hit several inches beyond the object.

So this is a strong use one of the visualization techniques that we were speaking of earlier and that is done during any and every workout as opposed to the type of visualization that is done away from the actual physical training locale.

Even when we are using weights that would prevent optimal speed (80 percent and above), we should still be making every effort to explode and move the bar as quickly as possible, taking advantage of the skills and mental imagery gained in the more dynamic training modes. That is really the whole point.

So, what else might be preventing us from applying 100 percent efforts in physical performance?

How about fear? Fear and doubt go hand in hand and will prevent a 100 percent effort every time they are allowed to manifest themselves unchecked.

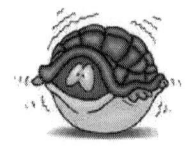

When faced with a daunting task such as squatting a massive weight or running a 100 yard dash as fast as possible, sometimes we let our minds wander into that dangerous zone of the negative **"what if"**? What if I tear a muscle? What if I lose my balance? What if the weights are unevenly loaded? What if I trip and fall? The list can go on and on, if we allow that line of thought to even get started.

One of the primary reasons that we must sometimes train with 1 rep max weights or run as fast as we can for a desired distance is to teach the mind to get used to this kind of an effort.

The subconscious mind does not like surprises. When we have physically "greased the groove" by repetitively doing a similar movement, we also have mentally "greased the groove". We have conditioned the mind to perform the movement without question or hesitation. Do a heavy single deadlift often enough and fear of doing a heavy single becomes a thing of the past, or at least it should. This is one reason I am not a fan of some lifting routines in which you never make any max or very close to max single attempts. While there is little doubt that doing higher reps builds strength, and many would say that doing a maximum effort single does little toward building strength, I tend to disagree with the idea that this means we should not be training with heavy singles. I would contend that though a percentage chart might tell you what your projected max single is, based upon having done x number of reps with a certain weight, if you have trained only with sets of 5s, triples or even doubles, your body will be "surprised" when it is saddled with a 1 rep max weight, and this is not a good thing. I think the same ideas hold true when it comes to other training modes, like running or other athletic endeavors that require an all out short duration burst. My point in all of this is that practicing for your maximum effort competitions by performing maximum effort training events will reduce and hopefully eliminate the fear factor when it comes time for that all out movement at crunch time. Also, this may seem counter-intuitive, but training near max singles in a given movement may be less traumatic to the musculature than performing multiple higher rep sets or even 1 all out set with a sub maximal weight. Think in terms of total tonnage involved. If for example I train the deadlift by warming up with relatively light weights and then start performing a series of singles, working up to a very high percentage of 1 rep max, the total tonnage will be less than it would have been had I done a series of higher rep sets and only worked up to a considerably smaller percentage of max. Another thing to consider about the "all-out" set with a lighter weight is that form often deteriorates as the set progresses and the last reps may get sloppy or even not fully completed. We can fool ourselves this way, believing we are capable of a certain 1 rep max rep based on the number of reps done in such an all out set, but it was not a legitimate set of whatever because the last rep or two were not done properly. Let's say the warm-up sets are exactly the same for the following 2 scenarios of rep schemes, up until reaching the 400 pound level. In both scenarios, 400 pounds is done for 1 rep only. In scenario number one, the weight will then be moved up to 500 pounds for a set of 5 reps. The total post warm-up tonnage is then 2500 pounds in scenario number 1. In scenario 2, we go from the 400 single to a 475 single, then to a 510 single, and finish with a 545 single. In the second scenario, the total tonnage is only 1530 pounds. I guaranty you will recover much more quickly from the second scenario scheme, yet your top set is of similar "value" in terms of the projected percentage of 1 rep max you have worked with.

You will also have "greased the groove", mentally searing into your sub conscious the feeling of performing a max or near max single.

You can do more volume when you do your explosive sub maximal training, with multiple sets of doubles or triples with a much lighter weight. Now, there are people that would be at odds with me on this kind of thinking, suggesting that max effort or near max effort singles are more taxing on the recovery systems and particularly on the CNS, especially when we talk about movements like squats and deadlifts. Also, one could make the argument that proper visualization training, in which the 1 rep max single is visualized rather than actually performed; it would prepare the mind for the job without subjecting the mind to the stress created by the physical event. It becomes a matter of preference and experimentation for each person as to where that line is drawn. Obviously, even if our visualization skills are highly tuned, as was the case with Maxick, whom we discussed earlier, we still must lift heavy weights in training at some point if we are to lift heavy weights in competition. The Westside guys train for heavy singles pretty often, but avoid the CNS burnout and lots of the physical trauma simply by switching the form of the exercises around frequently. They might use a different bar to squat with, change the stance, bar placement, use different combinations of bands and chains, etc. when doing max efforts.

They learned this to an extent from the original Westside crew, who switched from standard squats to box squats of varying heights on the squat, and often did heavy inclined benches, belly tosses or pad presses in place of straight up barbell benches. On the deadlift, lifting off large wood blocks or off pins from different positions in a power cage was done often in place of pulling from the floor. For much more in-depth coverage on the original guys, their concepts, training methods and personal stories & anecdotes, grab a copy of my book "**Forgotten Secrets of the Culver City Westside barbell club revealed**".

Now I'll grant you, the new version of the WS crew has a lot more tools at their disposal than the originals did, so they have really expanded on the concepts of which I write.

More lessons from the martial arts realm

I came across an article some time back when I was researching the whole concept of Ki or Chi that we just were discussing. The article is called "12 steps to developing Chi". Some of the steps involve things we have gone over already, so to keep from being too redundant, I'll take a few excerpts from the article that I feel are important to our subject.

Step 3

- An indomitable spirit can certainly contribute to the development of "**Chi**". With a leap of faith and the initiative to succeed at all cost, you can produce a spirit on fire. You believe in yourself and your abilities. Your spirit becomes alive Faith created, faith demonstrated, and faith reinforced can never be destroyed.

Your face has a healthy glow to it; your mind and body are filled with excitement. You don't anticipate your next move, you just do it, with flow, and ease, and confidence.

Step 4

The banishment of fear when performing or facing a certain task will contribute to the creation of a strong "**Chi**". I am not afraid, I can do this thing, and I can do it better than anyone else. With fear and stomach butterfly's gone, energy rises, strength increases, and power surges to every muscle, bone and sinew of your body. You move forward, afraid of nothing. Your only concern is the moment at hand; everything else is completely blanked out. You are not concerned about your surroundings or about the people around you. Everything falls into place and fits perfectly together as in a jigsaw puzzle.

Now, to accomplish this you must learn to control the "**Flight or Fight**" syndrome. Simply stated, when fear or danger comes upon you, you may choose to run, you may freeze and do nothing, or you may opt to fight back and stand your ground. In most cases, a well trained, well adjusted, mature martial artist will stand his/her ground, assess the fear, and make the correct decisions needed to handle or to diffuse the situation. Remember this point, someone with strong "**Chi**" will not fear sounds in the night, foggy evenings, monsters, or ogres, whoopees or wheepees, as investigation will always turn up a simple solution. Yes, it is always wise to be cautious, alert and on guard but, it is shameful and self destructive to be full of fear. Train your body, train your mind, train your spirit, be strong and be prepared. There is no fear, there are only bad situations and bad people that have to be dealt with.

First sentence in **Step 5:**

- A strong, realistic, vivid imagination can contribute to a stronger "**Chi**"

The start of **Step 7:**

- To gain strong" **Chi**" you must become an expert at what you do. The rule of thumb is **Practice, Practice, and Practice**. "**Chi**" is automatic, non-thinking, reflective action, muscle memory, timeless, powerful, and is part of your very soul. To do anything well you have to do it over and over until it becomes a part of your nature.

The article speaks much about the use of visualization, and about being very intentional about achieving your goals one step at a time.

Here is the author's summary:

SUMMARY

"**Chi**" can be developed by,

1. Building outer strength.
2. A balance between mind and body.
3. An indomitable spirit.
4. Banishing fear.
5. Developing a strong imagination.
6. Be an expert.
7. Adding excitement.
8. Using visualization.
9. Tuning into vibrations.
10. Being a person of peace.
11. Becoming a success.
12. Using what you are born with.

Now, in my humble opinion the part about tuning into vibrations goes a little off the reservation, speaking of telepathy and the like, but I think most of the rest of it offers some very sound ideas.

This footnote was also interesting:

> As a footnote, I believe that in years past it was easier to develop **"Chi"** than it is today because everything that a person received was done so by hard work and lean times. Today, much is given to our young folks on a silver platter. The word **"given"** means just that, no work, no struggle, no tested by fire.

This article was written by someone calling themselves SOKE, and was found online.

Our Martial Artist friends have some tried & true methods of "getting in the Zone", and I think there is much worthy of study in that regard, even if you have no interest in the actual fighting skills themselves. I think this is yet another proof that we must look to many genres and training disciplines, exploring their ideas to see if we can gain something useful from them even if we do not wish to become full-fledged practitioners of these particular disciplines.

Now, going back to mental training concepts from the weight training side: I am going to ad a very interesting older article I came across by one of the old school greats here:

Confidence is Half the Battle

By W.A. Pullum

Figure 13. Pullum, legendary weightlifter and record breaker.

You will recall Pullum mentioned earlier in the section about Max Sick and friends.

Confidence, 'tis said, is half the battle, and as this relates to supreme achievements at weightlifting, certainly this is so. To *expect* to do a thing, whatever it may be, sets to work the powers which make it possible under the best conditions. Frees them from the shackling handicap of ***half-hearted endeavor***, brought about by fears of hesitating uncertainty – ***products of an indecisive outlook***! Confidence to the extent of ***expecting success*** in the performance of a weightlifting feat is built, in the first place – ***or it should be*** – on factual knowledge subconsciously operating; knowledge that all bodily positions going to be assumed are automatically dependable. It then proceeds from ***belief*** – a state of mind arising from appreciation of ***apparent*** physical powers possessed at that moment, computed from the "feel" of the weight. Assuming technique dependable, ***this*** is the deciding factor. If the weight *feels* "liftable" it CAN be lifted. That is a factual presumption! As we are dealing now with matters of the mind, it is instructive to remark that all the greatest champions and record breakers that I have known, were (or are) men who never allowed themselves to be; ***hypnotized by poundage*** that is to say, to **be *intimidated*** by the figures of the weight. The only thing that influenced them was how it felt, according to their powers of the time.

Because of that, they seldom attempted feats which were beyond the bounds of possibility. For the really great champion lifter is not prone to kid himself; at least, not when "on the job."

Confidence – A Valuable Possession

Confidence has *several aspects which are worthy of study*. It not only manifests itself in the form of competent self-assurance, as this may be displayed in connection with the essay of some great weightlifting feat. Determination eventually to succeed with that feat, when it is first envisaged, can *build itself on an innate belief that the feat is ultimately possible*. Confidence can also be *the feeding force all the time responsible for the sustainment of staminal morale*. And without question, it plays a great part in the establishment of that particular faculty which I have dealt with in the past – the sense of balance! Confidence, in all its aspects, is a valuable possession, as by its use great achievements become possible in all walks of life. And no man has a better opportunity to develop this faculty within him than the thoughtfully reasoning weightlifter. As many men have discovered to their advantage – not confined to champions at that! This psychological byproduct of its practice is one of the things which make the Iron Game such a fascinating pursuit. The first of the five pictures illustrating this article is an example of *how* one thoughtfully reasoning weightlifter *successfully creates confidence within himself* for an attempt on something which otherwise would little or no confidence backing the effort.

It is a photograph of Jim Halliday about to essay a Press – a lift on which he does not shine *because of structural handicaps*. Study his position and general bearing, and it will be seen by anyone who understands these things that they represent confidence personified. That is because Jim has **positively "willed" himself to a confident outlook,** and the position he has taken up not only depicts this, but, as he knows – no one better – **will assist him as far as this is possible.**

LEFT—Jim strikes a confident starting attitude for his worst lift—the Press! For here he is seen training to develop confidence on this lift. CENTRE—The bell is on the way to be fixed at the chest without the assistance of split or dip. Another Halliday confidence-developing exercise. RIGHT—Plenty of confidence as well as strength is needed to take 150 lbs. from the floor to arms' length as Jim is here shown doing it. He is nevertheless working well within his power.

Just as it is very difficult for some great actors to be really anything but themselves, no matter how they are cast – their individual personalities being so strong, their various idiosyncrasies so marked – so it is equally difficult for an experienced lifter to **manufacture a belief** that his powers **are greater** than they would seem to be, **and confidently proceed on that assumption.**

Determination may impel him to try to make the superior essay, emotional stress (by its excitation of the nervous system) may temporarily supply the additional force and drive to make it possible. But it won't proceed from possibility to *certainty* unless a supremely confident belief is held in mind that the latter IS GOING TO BE SO!

Study Jim's Methods

Halliday has done such astonishing things in weightlifting – *under the most adverse conditions possible to conceive* – that an examination of his methods (so far as these can be legitimately disclosed) is evidently well worthwhile. One has only to remember the base from which he restarted lifting after the war – *3 ½ years in a Japanese prison camp* – to appreciate that these methods must be worthy of study, considering what they have since done for him, not only in the lifting sphere but the bodybuilding one also. Jim is a great believer in the practice of special "assistance exercises" for everything that comes within the orbit of his activities; *that particular type of exercise which I designed and so named in 40 years ago or more (-1910).* It would therefore be very strange if one found that in his curriculum there were not some included for the promotion of the confidence factor.

Something from Bulgaria, circa 1963:

**Psychological Preparation of Weightlifters
by Philip Guenov, Chief National Coach, Bulgaria (1963)**

The Russian General A. V. Suverov once said,

"The more sweat in training, the less blood in battle."

This is as true for weightlifters as it is for soldiers, though we would have to substitute "failure in competition" for "blood in battle." Training hard, sometimes under deliberately unfavorable conditions as sometimes arise in competition, develops the weightlifter's persistence and tenacity, his will power. Sometimes the training quarters should be noisy and sometimes a bent bar should be used.

Sometimes the lifter should have to wait awhile to take his turn, to see how he reacts to cooling off while other men make their attempts.

A strict self-discipline in personal living habits also is important in training, for giving up pleasures strengthens the will and diminishes drains on both psychic and physical resources. For example, the Russian heavyweight champion Medvedev never used alcohol or tobacco and never missed a workout – not even to the extent of being late – during 15 years of competition.

BOLDNESS AND RESOLUTION

To succeed against his opponents in competition, a weight lifter should be bold and resolute. By this I mean he must have the capacity for quick and correct moves in complete confidence – without any hesitation, doubts or fears.

Hesitation and doubt are the greatest psychological enemies of lifters.

They lead to fear of the weight and failure, which in turn reinforces the hesitation and doubt in a vicious cycle. The coach can help overcome these handicaps by explaining what he must do in tones of complete confidence that he will be able to do it. There are a number of things a coach can do to instill confidence in a lifter. Suppose for example, a lifter has done 330 lbs. in the Clean & Jerk several times and it is obvious to the coach that he has the potential to lift 340. But the lifter himself is unsuccessful in making the increase because he doubts himself and is afraid of the weight. To convince him that he is capable of lifting the heavier weight the coach might do the following: If the lifter doubts he can **clean** the weight, the coach might have him assume the low split or squat position and have training partners hand him not 340, but 350 or 360 lbs., and stand by him to "spot" him while he proves to himself that he can recover with an ever heavier weight than he is afraid of. If he doubts that he can **jerk** the weight, the coach might have him support 350 lbs. overhead in the split jerk position and recover from it, and hold even heavier weights at his chest and overhead in the solid finishing position to make him feel that the weight he has been afraid of is in reality a "light" weight.

These techniques can, of course, be applied to other movements and disciplines as well.

A particularly great obstacle to be overcome is an established record, be it personal or competitive. Faced with the possibility of breaking a record, a lifter may fail because of psychological stresses. He may think of the difficulty of doing what he, or no one else, has ever done before. He may think of the fame and feeling of well-being that will come to him if he succeeds, of the reactions of family and friends, and of his opponents. The many distracting thoughts that come to the mind of an athlete trying to break a record disturb the balance of his painstakingly learned lessons. Emotions disturb his learned patterns of movement and sap his will to succeed. Because of this, the movement is executed incorrectly, with unnecessary stiffness and strain. His coordination is destroyed and the attempt is unsuccessful.

About record attempts, M. Ozolin has said,

"Even the highest records must be stormed simply, without any bending before them, (the athlete) relying only on himself." Tommy Kono spoke in a similar vein: "The aim of the lifter must be directed at world records and beyond them. He must strive not for individual and national achievements, but against world records.

He must progress steadily and he must train with heavy weights." Regularly striving to lift heavier and heavier weights not only builds strength, but also the confidence that the lifter can move on, so that boldness and resolution becomes a habit that remains with him when he attempts to break a record.

THE EFFECT OF AN OPPONENT

A weight lifter competes not only with the weight, but also against his opponents. Many well-trained athletes who have the strength and skill to win are defeated psychologically when they become overawed by the reputation of a competitor. On the other hand, an athlete may be defeated by a weaker opponent because he underestimates him and expects an easy victory. Overconfident, he may fail to complete a lift, which may give his opponent the inspiration he needs to outdo his previous best and win the contest. Here is an example: At the Rome Olympics, Ike Berger was considered a sure winner. Minaev was assigned the modest responsibility of trying to place second. But Berger failed twice to press 231 lbs. and only succeeded on his third attempt. Minaev suddenly realized that the gold medal was within his reach. He became a new man, bold and inspired, and did his best lifting in the snatch and jerk so that to beat him Berger needed to clean & jerk 336 lbs. This would have broken the world record by 11 lbs. Berger had actually lifted this much in training, but now he was unnerved by falling behind and by the confident attitude of Minaev, and he failed. Another example: Vorobyev was for years an undefeated world champion and record holder. But in the 1959 world championships he lost his title to Louis Martin of Great Britain, who was competing in a world championship for the first time. Vorobyev held the world record for total and even when not at his best seemed capable of 1,000 lbs. Martin's previous best total was 945. In the championships, Vorobyev was troubled by an injury from which he had not fully recovered and, as he failed with lifts he should have been able to make, Martin became inspired, succeeding with a clean & jerk of 386 lbs. and tied Vorobyev's total of 980.

Martin was the lighter man and knew he could win by lifting the 386 so with boldness and resolution he succeeded.

These examples show how important it is for lifters to know the performances and potentialities of their opponents. Realizing this, we maintain a bulletin board with the names, photographs, and lifting results of our competitors.

Thus our lifters learn to oppose their competitors and to develop the determination to defeat them. They try to defeat their opponents on the bulletin board all year 'round. Other factors that must be considered in preparing an athlete to go through a contest with resolution and boldness are the conditions of the contest itself. Training situations should sometimes involve an audience, lifting at the time of day or night the contest will be held, noise, lighting, and the long delays that almost invariably occur.

Simulating contest conditions will help the athlete prepare himself for distractions that might otherwise interfere with his psychological readiness to do his best.

SELF-MASTERY

Another important volitional quality is that of self-control. The lifter must not be thrown off balance by an unexpected failure or an unexpected success by his opponent. As an example of how a lifter was able to keep from being discouraged, consider the experience of Yuri Vlasov the first time he competed in a world championship: In the press, Vlasov succeeded with 352 lbs. instead of the 374 he expected to lift and had been lifting successfully in training. His opponent, Jim Bradford, took a big lead by pressing 390 lbs. Vlasov did not allow himself to be discouraged. Maintaining great self-mastery, he flawlessly snatched 325 lbs. and jerked 424 to overcome the deficit and win the world championship. As another example, at the 1960 European championships Ivan Vesselinov, of Bulgaria, was able to overcome a series of failures by iron-willed self-mastery. Vesselinov missed his first attempt in the press and was unable to press any more than his starting weight. To make the best possible total, he took his first attempt in the snatch with his personal record of 286 lbs. – and failed! Instead of giving up, Vesselinov returned to the platform with new resolve and succeeded on his second try. Then he went on to snatch 297 on his third attempt, establishing a Bulgarian national record. But his troubles were still far from over.

In his first attempt at the clean and jerk, with 386 lbs., he fell under the bar and was slightly injured. Ignoring his bruises, Vesselinov determinedly returned to the platform and lifted the 386 and then went on to establish another Bulgarian record by cleaning and jerking 408 lbs! Such self-mastery as was shown by Vlasov and Vesselinov is only possible, of course, when it is backed by much hard work in training. This is why the final training periods should employ the same type of activity as will be experienced in the actual contest. More work should be done with the three Olympic lifts, in order, and with very heavy weights. In the last few days before the contest, of course, the lifter must taper off with the very heavy work in order to build a reserve of nervous energy. It sometimes happens that a lifter will fail twice with his starting weight in a contest. Realizing that he must succeed on his third try, or lose all chance for personal success or to help his team, the lifter is under great nervous tension as he makes his final attempt. In an attempt to overcome this, we often ask an athlete to lift a limit weight, or five or 10 lbs. less than his limit, during training while imagining that he has failed twice and must now succeed in order to make a total and save his team from defeat. It is up to the coach to take a lifter aside after failure and reassure and encourage him. The coach must persuade him by his tone of voice and attitude as well as his words that the lifter can and **will** succeed on his next attempt. It is a good idea to do the same in training, instead of letting the lifter drop back to a light weight if he really seems capable of handling the weight he has failed with. The coach must also be alert for complacency and over-confidence in a lifter who has just succeeded very well with one or both of the first two lifts. The lifter must not be permitted to consider the contest won or the training session over until the last lift has been made.

FIRMNESS OF WILL

Firmness of will, or will power, is needed by a lifter in order to do his best despite feeling tired and weary of competition. With strong will power, he will be able to dominate his feelings of fatigue. Often you will see a lifter fail with a clean & jerk toward the end of a long contest even though the weight is one he has lifted successfully in training or in smaller contests. Professor Mateev says fatigue diminishes the activity of nerve cells in the cortex of the brain, so that exact coordination suffers and reaction time decreases. By great exercise of will power, an athlete can increase the activity of these cells so that he regains the nervous energy needed to force his muscles to perform up to the level of strength they are capable of. **Thus a lifter should strengthen his will power by occasionally lifting maximal weights in training when he feels tired.** If he is unwilling to try, his coach should exhort him to go on and even criticize him in front of other members of the team if this stimulus is needed to make him keep trying. Firmness of will also included the ability to overcome negative emotions – fear, despair, difference, and so on. The only way a lifter can truly learn to overcome these and other unsuspected difficulties that will crop up during competition is by experiencing competition itself. Only participating in contests can create the situation of highest possible attention for the lifter, in which he can strengthen his volitional qualities. Therefore lifters should enter competition regularly, especially against opponents who are at about their level of performance, where they will be called upon to do their best in order to place or win. A lifter does not improve by competing where he can win easily, nor will it do his morale any good to be competing always against men who are far above his level.

Author's note

Obviously the above article was focused on Olympic lifting, but I think we can take some of the lessons from it and use them for any desired goal

Some more wisdom from a very prolific writer:

The Correct Mental Approach
by Charles A. Smith (1954)

That great champion and strength athlete, **Tommy Kono**, world record holder in several divisions, is responsible for a story that is now part of weightlifting history. Tommy was also a pretty good bodybuilder. When asked how he managed to lift such enormous poundage at his comparatively low bodyweight, instead of pointing to his muscles, or attributing his success to some magic formula, exercise, or training program or technique, Tommy tapped his forehead and said . . . **"It's all in the mind."**

The majority of the people in the crowd standing around him lost the significance of the remark entirely, but the few who did grasp it were more than fully aware of what Tommy meant and how right he was.

It is possible for a man to possess every physical lifting requirement . . . strength . . . speed . . . good technique, yet fail utterly to progress as a lifter simply because he lacks some essential mental quality.

TOMMY KONO is a very meticulous lifter. He walks deliberately to the bar and always measures his hands spacing carefully from the center of bar.

Above you see Tommy's great physique (Tommy is on the left)

For a man must not only be suited physically to lifting, he must also be of a certain disposition.

There's no real need for me to give you any examples. You've all seen men who can make a first attempt with ridiculous ease, then fail to negotiate an increase of ten pounds; whose lifting is erratic; good form one day, falling to pieces on another for no apparent reason. You've met scores of athletes who can lift far greater poundage in training than they've ever accomplished in competition. There are others who are so full of confidence before an attempt, which then go all haywire when the actual moment arrives. There are men who reach championship form and poundage in a local contest, yet fail to come anywhere near these performances when they have to compete against tough opponents.

I personally know a heavyweight who could have been the greatest lifter in his class the world has ever seen. Long ago, if it wasn't for his temperament, he could have gone way beyond a 1050 total in the three Olympic lifts and easily reached the fabulous 1100 aggregate. But his habit of indulging in self-pity, of sinking into the depths of despair, of regarding himself as a total failure each time he had an off day in training, but paid to his career. On the other hand, there have been scores of lifters, and not all of them necessarily world champions, who have made the grade when on the surface they had hardly any of the attributes people associate with a successful weightlifter.

Thin, weak when they began lifting, they still managed to rise to their best because of an indefinable mental factor.
Some people call it the will to win. Others say it is determination. Some say it is keeping cool, calm and collected, while others maintain it is knowing what you want and letting nothing get in your way, subordinating everything to the task of reaching your goal.

But no matter by what names these mental requirements of lifting are known, it is possible to develop them if they are lacking, and increase them if they are present. The time to start is now, not in a day's time, or a week, or a month, but now, right now as you are reading these words.

Take that thin edge of the wedge of your determination to be a better lifter, thrusting itself under the doubts that are preventing you from making the most of your physical qualities. Repeat these words to yourself when you get up in the morning, when you go to bed at night, before and after you take a workout . . .

"There's nothing that will stop me from becoming a good lifter." (Read; good runner, wrestler, football player, crossfitter, etc)

Don't let any doubts enter your mind. You are going to succeed. You ARE going to make good progress. You WILL reach your goals. And you realize that there will be obstacles to overcome, that there will be setbacks, times when your progress will level, halt for a while. But despite it all you will rise and succeed. There's one rule you must follow in your training and here it is. Set a definite day once a month, when you will make limit attempts.

On that day and at no other times, try yourself out. Here's why. Just as certain physical aspects of lifting are influenced by mental attitude and approach to problems, so the mind can also be influenced by habitual action of the body. If you constantly try 200 lbs. in the clean and never succeed, you will build up a pattern of failure as normal. The wisest course for you to follow is to stay comfortably below your limit, while handling the necessary heavy weights to build combined power and technique. **Don't let your friends kid you into making fruitless efforts to lift a weight which you know is above your strength.** Keep to a once-a-month tryout, and then if you fail to lift the weight you made the previous month, you will not be disturbed by this and you will not build up any bad habit patterns. You will simply tell yourself that you know you have made the weight before, but tonight you're just a little off form, going through a stale period. Don't discount the value of Basic Power exercises since these have as deep a mental influence as they have physical. Here's one experiment you can try to provide this. Take a weight 10 lbs. below your press or jerk limit. Hold it at the shoulders for a short period, then place it on the ground. Then take a barbell 50-100 lbs. above your press or jerk, and hold it across the shoulders for as long as possible. Put it down and take up the first weight again. Notice how light it feels now, as if you could perform rep after rep with it. After working on your regular lifts, use basic power exercises such as heavy, high deadlifts, high pull ups, partial bench presses, etc., etc. These will accustom the muscles to handle the heaviest weights, strengthen the tendons and ligaments, and give a feeling of "lightness" to your press, clean, etc. All great lifters use or have used these movements and all obtain great benefit from them . . . mental as well as physical. In the gym or in a contest, never allow the reputation of other lifters to scare you. Go in knowing just what you are capable of and just what you intend to lift. If there are other men who can outlift you, recognize this fact but be determined to do your best and more if possible. *You may not be the strongest man in the gym, or win first place in a contest, but tell yourself that your turn is surely coming.*

Don't get nervous about the outcome when lifting. Just picture in your mind exceeding yourself, of giving a sterling performance, of letting the other men see that you are a man to be reckoned with in the future. Do all you can to make yourself acceptable as a lifter, by behaving in a sportsmanlike manner at all times.

Remember that physical performance and nervous energy, are both stimulated by the mind.

I have seen Pete George pacing up and down at the back of the platform whipping himself into a frenzy with his intense concentration, his driving will to succeed at a lift. Tommy Kono goes through the same process, as does Dave Shephard, Stan Stanczyk and Norbert Schemansky.

Norbert

What does the "working up" accomplish? It produces tremendous bursts of explosive energy, which are quite beyond the athlete normally, and because of these energy bursts and stimulation the lifter is capable of making poundage that was previously impossible for him.

It means that the adrenal glands work overtime, as they always do in times of great excitement, danger, or when great muscular output is required, and the outpouring of the marvel hormone, adrenalin, into the blood stream makes a greater muscular effort possible . . . but possible only because of the prior mental stimulation.

Don't take too long over an attempt. The more you hang around the longer you have to imagine how heavy the weight is.

Whatever you do, don't start thinking about how hard you'll have to pull, how much weight is on the bar, how heavy the last attempt felt, and how difficult this one's gonna be. That will encourage a negative approach and lead to certain failure, because you will be concerned more with the possibility of failing than succeeding.

Here's what you have to do to combat this. Before you make the attempt, picture in your mind exactly how you are going to tear that barbell off the ground and overhead to arms' length, how you are certain to rise from a squat without hesitation, how that bar will fly from your chest to lockout. Convince yourself that there's absolutely nothing to prevent you from making a perfect lift and a new personal record.

When your turn comes to make an attempt, stand over the bar. Say something to yourself like "Here's where I show them what a real snatch is." Go over the pull from both feet, the flight of the bar straight up the body, the fast split off the platform, both feet at the same time, the lightning-like drop of the body under the bar, the easy, sure recovery and then . . . tear that weight to arms' length!

Follow the same mental pattern when attempting any lift; Positive, Confident, Flawless performance.

The only way you can become a good lifter is to make yourself the master of your muscles. Rule your lifting actions, know what you are going to do and then go right ahead and do it. Some years ago, a young man joined the Bronx Union YMCA, where I was instructing at the time. He joined for the purpose of having me teach him Olympic lifting style, he told me. ***He was tall, slender, not particularly powerful, a run-of-the-mill lifter but for one thing . . . his incredible will to win.*** That man was so filled with determination to succeed, was so certain that he had the potential to be a great lifter that ***others often thought he was kidding himself.*** But he knew what he wanted. He ruled his training with an iron will.

He never considered the possibility of failure and he went from triumph to triumph.

Today, Herbie Schiff, late of the Bronx and now living in California, is one of the greatest heavyweights in the world, totaling 980 lbs. and ***all because he thought only of succeeding and never of failing!***

Here is a great article found online a while back with some solid tips:

The Power of Positive Lifting

Russian Revelation

In 1979, Dr. Charles Garfield, a good friend of mine and weight lifter, met with a group of Soviet sports psychologists and physiologists in Milan. They told him about the phenomenal effects of intense mental training on athletic performance. After spending several days with the Soviet researchers, Garfield had heard enough theory. He wanted to see results. At a gym, the Soviets quizzed Garfield. "How long since you've done any serious training?" they asked. "Eight years." "What was your maximum bench press in your prime?" "365 pounds." "In recent years what is the most you've pressed?" "280 pounds." It intrigued the Soviets that Garfield had once pressed 365. "How long would you have to train to make that lift again?" they asked. "Nine to twelve months," he said. The Soviet doctors then asked him, "Would you attempt a 300-pound lift right now?" Garfield reluctantly agreed to try. Spurred and encouraged by the Russians, and much to his surprise,

Garfield (barely) made the lift. Then the Soviet doctors went to work. They guided him into a state of deep relaxation for 40 minutes. Then they added 65 pounds to the 300. They had him visualize approaching the bar, lying on the bench and confidently making the lift. They told him to imagine each phase of the lift: the sound of the jangling weights, his breathing, the noises of exertion he ordinarily made when lifting. Garfield got nervous, certain he couldn't do it. He began to worry about even pressing 300 again. But the Soviets calmly told him to visualize lifting the 365. They had him look closely at his hands, the weights, and said to imagine how his muscles would feel after he succeeded. As they talked him through the whole process again, the series of images, and then the total picture, began to clarify in Garfield's mind. "The imagery now imprinted in my mind began to guide my physical movements . . . The world around me seemed to fade, giving way to self-confidence, belief in myself and then to deliberate action.

"I lifted the weights!"*

Garfield had learned two important concepts in the power of mental training: ***concentration and visualization***. It's a lesson that more and more athletes are using to their advantage.

Sports Psychology

Stress is real. Physiologically, the pulse quickens, the breathing rate changes. A relief pitcher in a tight spot feels it. A sprinter in the starting blocks feels it. A bodybuilder feels it before posing. ***It's a mistake to deny stress and the energy it creates***. All of us have "choked" — tensed up under pressure. It may not have been in sports, but there have been times when the "heat" of a stressful situation has shot you down. When this happens, it means the anxiety is out of control. You lose concentration and can't direct your attention. It doesn't have to be that way.

You can use stress to your advantage.

Stress keeps you alert; it prods you into being more productive. It's a challenge to control your responses to stressful situations, but it's a challenge you can win. In sports, wholeness is essential. ***The most physically skilled competitor who ties up mentally will be unsuccessful.*** Until very recently, the mind/body integration and awareness so crucial for athletic success had been ignored in training for most sports. Now, taking a cue from the Soviets and East Germans, who pioneered the emphasis on holistic training, athletes work on the mental aspect of training as well as the physical.

Knowing that you can control your behavior and your response to stress gives you a great boost in confidence.

There are strategies and skills you can learn which help keep your thoughts positive and constructive, dissipate needless tension, and redirect your attention when you do have a mental lapse. Let's get more specific.

Accentuate the Positive

The key to success in anything is to rehearse success rather than rehearse failure.

All athletes must contend with negative thinking. It can be caused by previous negative experiences, the negative thoughts of others, or your own self-doubts. A friend of mine, Dan, played basketball for a U.S. Navy team. In one game, Dan was at the foul line with only a few seconds left to play. His team trailed by a point. If he made the two free throws they would win. To increase pressure on Dan, the opposing coach called a time-out. During the time-out, Dan started "rehearsing failure," thinking what a goat he'd be if he missed. Dan's coach saw the state he was in. "Look, Dan," he said, "You're the best free-throw shooter on the team. There's no one I'd rather have shooting. Make the shots, be a hero and let's go home." Dan made both shots.

The coach had successfully redirected Dan's negative energy into a positive pattern. Here's a simple way to practice accentuating the positive: Keep your workouts upbeat.

Positive thinking is not only for competitions. Work on positive thoughts the same way you work on your body — all the time.

Think positive thoughts in practice. "*The world looks good. I'm glad I'm training today. I feel great.*" Avoid thoughts like, "Things keep piling up around me." Or, "I'll never get things done properly." Remember that your training session is probably the only time you'll have all day that's just for you. You want it to be as pleasant, positive and productive as possible.

The Athletes' Guide to Sports Psychology (Leisure Press, 1984) deals with "mental skills for physical people." It has a long list of negative thoughts and their positive counterparts. Here are a few:

Negative Thoughts	***Change to Positive Thoughts***
I can't.	I can do it. I have done it many times before.
I am tired, I can't go on.	The hardest part is almost over, I know I can finish.

I am getting worse instead of better.	I will set daily goals and evaluate my progress on a regular basis.
The heat is so bad I cannot do anything.	The heat creates a greater challenge.
I am really nervous and anxious.	The last time I felt this way I performed my best.
I am afraid that I will make a fool of myself.	Unless I face the challenge and take the risk, I'll never know what I can accomplish
I don't want to fail.	What is the worst thing that could happen? I could lose. If so, I will work harder the next time around.
I don't think I am	I have practiced and trained hard for this

prepared.	performance so I am prepared to do well.
I lost again. I'll never be a winner.	I can learn from losing. I need to talk with a coach to get some help regarding those things I need to improve.
It is not fair. I work just as hard as _____ but don't do as well.	I may have to work harder than some to get to the same level. I will work as hard as I have to because I want to succeed.
I never seem to be able to do this.	This time I am going to think it through and mentally prepare to do it.

Concentration

In July 1985, John Howard set the world land speed record for bicycles of 152 mph (drafting behind a race car). "I was very absorbed," said Howard. "My main concentration was on what was on the road in front. A helicopter was 10 feet above me, and I have no recollection of it. An atomic bomb could have exploded 1000 yards away and I wouldn't have known."

Top performance occurs when you focus on a goal, ignoring the distractions on the sidelines. You narrow the band of attention to the task at hand:

Hitting the pitch, catching the pass, or lifting the weight. It's like tuning in a radio station; ***you want to eliminate the static.***

Note: You don't need to concentrate intensely all the time. You can burn out mentally just as you can physically. A runner does not concentrate on form every time he trains. Sometimes he just runs for the joy of it. Likewise in lifting, you don't need to use visualization for each rep of each set. Save it for the last few reps of your key exercises. To maintain the power of intense concentration, you must do it at selected times, not every time you work out. Once you develop the knack, you save it for those special times. When you need it, it will be there.

Imagery

Imagery or visualization is the technique that helped Charlie Garfield lift 365 pounds. It's used by many athletes today and can help you achieve your goals. I used my own version of imagery in 1971 when preparing for the Mr. Universe contest.

I knew that Arnold Schwarzenegger would be my main competition, so I got the best possible photos of Arnold and taped them to my bathroom mirror. As I shaved each morning, here was Arnold in peak condition looking at me. Nose to nose with him, I'd tell myself, "I'm going to beat this guy." I carried these thoughts with me everywhere. At meals, I'd tell myself that the food I ate was making me stronger, leaner, less prone to injury. And that it would help me beat Arnold. When I went to sleep, I'd concentrate on the sleep making me a stronger, better person and athlete. And that this deep relaxing sleep would help me beat Arnold. In the end, Arnold withdrew from the competition. But I was ready and won the title. Herschel Walker, the great running back, uses visualization in his training:

"My mind's like a general and my body's like an Army. I keep the body in shape and it does what I tell it to do. I sometimes even feel myself almost lifting up out of my body and looking down on myself while I run sprints. I'll be coaching myself from up above. 'Come on, Herschel . . . pick up those knees. Pump your arms!'"

Bruce Morris of Marshall University in Huntington, West Virginia, made the longest field goal in college basketball history — 89' 10". Morris said, "All I could see was the rim, the basket, and the backboard. It seemed real close . . . it didn't seem that far away when I did it." Janet Evans, a woman who won three gold medals for swimming in 1988, a gold and silver at the Barcelona Games in 1992, and won the World Championship in 1993 said, "I continue to visualize all my races days and weeks before they happen . . .

I have never been to a competition, including the Olympic Games, where I didn't see myself win in my mental images before I got there. It is just part of the whole training package."

Tommy Moe, Olympic gold medalist in downhill skiing at Lillihammer, Norway said,

"I always picture myself on the victory podium when I practice my races, so that I can't imagine ending up anywhere else."

Danny Everett, 1988 Olympic gold medalist who set the world record in the 400 meters and broke the 1990 indoor world record in the 400-meter race in Stuttgart, Germany said, "During the race I felt like I wasn't even moving fast . . . It felt like a comfortable jog around the track. It was easy; there was no struggle, and I felt a floating quality to the race . . . almost like I was in slow motion. I felt like I had been to that race in Stuttgart in those weather conditions in my mind already . . . I looked up and couldn't believe my time. It didn't feel like a world record."

An excellent book on the subject is *Mental Training for Peak Performance* by Steven Ungerleider (Rodale Press, Emmaus, PA, 1996).

The above article excerpts are primarily geared towards Olympic lifting, but the principles involved can translate to powerlifting or any other sport you might wish to apply it to.

You see that visualization is a common theme; it is used greatly by many of those that excel in sports as well as in other areas of life. One of the beautiful aspects of using visualization is that **it is a great way to practice your sport skills without the possibility of physical injury or stress**. Again, remember that a properly executed session of visualization training is etched into the memory just like an actual physical training session, but sans the associated wear and tear on the body.

Summing it all up

As a 53 year old powerlifter that gave up steroids many years ago, getting additional training sessions in without the need for the recuperation that is normally required afterwards is a very appealing concept. The proper attitude and mental focus is only one part of the total training/health equation, but it is not one to be overlooked. **The combination of hard but smart physical training, solid nutrition and recuperative measures and mental training is the ticket to your best gains and ultimate performance.** Speaking of recuperation, this is another area in which visualization and other mental techniques can and should play a vital role. You have surely heard that people with a positive attitude recover from cancer and other illnesses at a considerably higher rate than those with a less positive view. Feeding your mind positive imagery and thoughts while performing self massage and other recuperation and rehabilitation methods will only enhance the outcome of such methods. Some folks would write off this kind of thinking as pschyco-babble. If you buy into that, then for you it might as well be just that; babble. One area that focuses on this kind of thing is Meridian tapping, which I mentioned in passing earlier, also known as EFT. Based on the same concepts used by those who perform acupressure and acupuncture, this method is founded on the idea that there are certain meridians or channels of energy that flow through the body in relatively defined pathways. Using certain key points along these pathways, one gently taps repeatedly on one at a time while feeding the mind positive thoughts in the form of a self-styled script designed to bring about the desired physical and/ or mental results. While some might associate some sort of meta-physical aspect to these methods, I do not. I have experimented with these methods and found them to be a good way to get into a relaxed state and the tapping seems to promote a calm and physically regenerative effect. I will admit that I don't exactly understand how or why it works, but do I really need to? The fact that it does work, at least to some extent, is good enough for me.

The following description and the chart showing tap points was provided by my friend Royce from an exercise forum we both frequent. He is a practitioner of a bodyweight exercise form known as Qi Gong.

Some schools of Qi Gong feature various forms of "meridian tapping." There are a variety of protocols, but some of the contemporary approaches combine specific affirmations to be used while tapping on selected meridian points in the body. Meridian tapping is a powerful and effective technique that can be utilized for a wide range of issues—emotional and physical. Frequent and repeated use of tapping can and should become an integral part of one's regimen for optimizing physical and mental capabilities. The tapping should be done on a regular basis for a wide range of issues. Establishing tapping sequences particularly suited for a given individual can be a very involved process, so this brief treatise should only be thought of a jumping off point for one to prepare for more advanced study.

Marked below are the key meridian points that one should focus upon:

Tapping Points

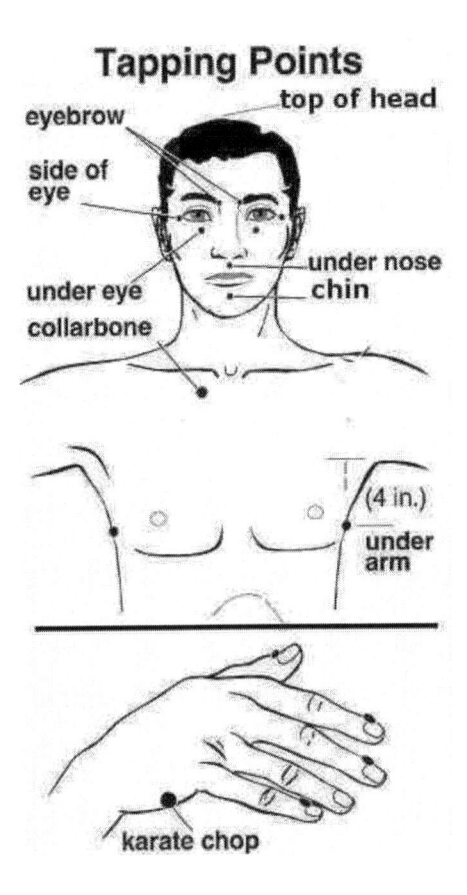

- eyebrow
- top of head
- side of eye
- under nose
- under eye
- chin
- collarbone
- (4 in.) under arm
- karate chop

All of the above points can be used; however, we can usually dispense with all of the hand points with the exception of one, and that key exception is the karate chop point. That is a tapping point that is uniquely important. Here are some examples of affirmations that can be done while tapping:

Fear:

(In this example, we will use the fear of public speaking. (Substitute other things most pertinent to you as an individual.) Remember to always start the tapping round with the karate chop point. "Even though I am terrified to speak in front of people, I deeply and completely have confidence in and accept myself anyway". "Even though I can feel my face heating, my breathing constricting and my fear growing, I deeply and completely have confidence in and accept myself." And for the third round: "Even though I can imagine standing in front of a group and saying something stupid that will cause them to lose respect for me, I will continue to deeply and completely have confidence in and accept myself anyway". Tap at least five times on each point listed in the chart for a complete round, and then repeat for at least three rounds. For our purposes in this book, we can use a script of a more physical nature, like:

"I have worked out hard today, and now my muscles and nervous system will relax and recuperation will be full". "I will be stronger for my next workout and will enjoy breaking new ground"

or something along these lines, simply repeated along with the tapping sequence already described. I thought I would present these as an inexpensive and fairly simple alternative to acupuncture or acupressure techniques. The various affirmations should be done intuitively and specific to one's special needs. Although discussions about various affirmations could fill volumes, the essential beginning sequence remains the same. Of course, there are other ways to combine mental training with rehab, prehab and recuperation technique. In a very simple way, you can just tell yourself things like:

My muscles are becoming stronger and more resilient and flexible by applying this self massage (plug in whatever therapy you happen to be using here)

I will fully recuperate from that last training session

(Be more specific here) and will be stronger for the next session

I am helping oxygen rich and nutrient filled blood get into every fiber of my muscles and connective tissues so that they will grow more powerful.

My healing will be full and complete as I continue to provide it with everything it needs to accelerate the process.

You get the idea, right?

Make up your own little "mantra" or script as you go along, or write something down and memorize it for repeated use. Or find someone else's that seems to fit your goals and desires. You can use similar "scripts" and "mantras" while performing self massage, cryotherapy, administering liniment, etc. I like the idea of "active rest". Sound like an oxymoron? It really isn't. While there is certainly a time and a place for inactive rest, like when you are sleeping, you can help your body recuperate better and faster by engaging in some moderate exercise, like light recumbent biking for example. "Mobility drills" have been around for a long time, though they have not always been called that. Doing arm circles with no weight, step-ups, kicks and things like this on "off days" can get blood pumping into the previously trained areas and facilitate healing.

Some words of inspiration from Man Factor/ Men of Destiny's Joe Anderson:

Subject: THERE IS NO SUCCESS WITHOUT HARDSHIP
The world is so constructed that if you wish to enjoy its pleasures, you must also endure its pains. Like it or not, you cannot have one without the other. Success is not measured by what you accomplish. It's measured by the opposition you encounter, and the courage with which you maintain your struggle against the odds. You'll find all things are difficult before they are easy. The greater your obstacles, the more glory in overcoming them. So, make up your mind before you start that sacrifice is part of the package. No pain, no gain; No thorns, no throne; No cross, no crown. You've got to go through the negative before you get to the positive.

More from Joe

DESIRE IS THE STARTING POINT OF SUCCESS **The first thing that will contribute to reaching your goal is that you simply want to reach it badly enough. You must learn how to desire with sufficient intensity to be successful. If you have the desire you have the power to attain success. You can really have anything you want in life if you go after it.**

"In Romania, I train on a bar that is bent. My gym has bad lighting and very little heat in the winters. Here in America, you have everything you need to train. It's not in the bar or the gym or the platform . . . *it's in you*."

Nicu Vlad

Becoming Versus Staying Motivated

The first step in better understanding motivation is to realize that there is an important distinction between becoming motivated and *staying* motivated. Becoming motivated is really pretty easy. I become motivated when I see someone really putting out in the gym, when I pick up a lifting book or magazine, after a run of a couple of outstanding workouts, or when I receive compliments on what I've done. All of these sources inspire me to greater efforts. However, the really challenging thing is learning how to stay motivated in training, especially when those nice positive outside stimuli are not around. Staying motivated is a major key in putting in consistent workouts. Staying motivated is less influenced by situational occurrences such as receiving compliments or reading a magazine. It has its base in one's *attitudes, beliefs, and goals*.
So, the critical issue of motivation is learning how to stay up for every workout. There is nothing magical about it.

Staying motivated is a learned habit that takes a little awareness and effort, but pays dividends in providing consistent and regular results. In order to better understand how to stay motivated in your training, take a little time now and answer this question: "What things do I need to regularly do, be, or have in order to stay motivated in my lifting?"

?

Some of you may have responded with such answers as good equipment, a regular training partner, previous successful workouts, appropriate and obtainable goals, good nutrition, intense concentration, or persistence. If you look at the types of answers you gave, you will notice that they usually fall into two general categories: those sources outside of you and those inside of you.

The Two Forms of Motivation

Successful lifters and bodybuilders understand that there are two forms of motivation: *extrinsic* (external) and *intrinsic* (internal). Each form is necessary in order to achieve consistent gains, but as in cooking, one has to know when to use each ingredient . . .

Visualizing a Lift: Before, After, Here, or There?

Visualization is the mental act of rehearsal. It is creating or recreating a lift in our imagination. This includes daydreaming, fantasizing, and guided tours in La-La Land. In our case, it's picturing the successful completion of a lift. It's positive thinking. Sports science has taught us that visualization electrically activates the corresponding muscle groups. Professional athletes and their coaches acknowledge the utility and importance of visualization in performance. Mental rehearsal can boost your performance because of the mind/body connection. Your mind as well as your muscles must learn and rehearse motor skills to maximize performance. The psychology and programming of visualization goes much deeper than what is presented here. This article will serve as a small taste of a practical idea. For more information, find a sports psychologist, life coach, or specialist familiar with these mental skills.

The <u>barbell</u> was heavy and intimidating

In 2010, I started barbell training. New to max effort lifts, I experienced great anxiety on 'find your 1RM' days. I just wanted the lifts to be over. I wanted all moments to exist except for the one where I was in the lift, doing the lift, and holding the bar. However, I think the one rep max is one of the coolest training ideas. The Sisyphean task of pursuing ever greater one rep maxes ranks above all else in my mind. Even now, though my programming has changed and my barbell knowledge and experience has expanded, I still hold the act of finding 'the heaviest single' to be the primal element of strength and power training. What helped me through these lifts and eased my anxiety was the use of visualization. As each session passed and I gained experience, I had more sensory information to draw from to enrich my visualizations, to make them more real. As I gained experience, I learned to be 'in the moment' and enjoy it.

This emotionally positive approach helped me gain further awareness—even and especially from the failed attempts.

Before, after, here, or there?

When you visualize a lift, you can do it in different ways. You can be associated or dissociated (here or there), and you can also visualize the process or the result (before or after). If you visualize your lifts and see everything through your own eyes as in reality, you're associated. You're visualizing in the first person. If you imagine your lifts from outside of your body, like watching yourself on television, you're dissociated. You're visualizing in the third person. When you visualize a lift and you only see the end, you're visualizing the results. For example, if you are about to snatch and you visualize the bar overhead, you're seeing the results. If you visualize what the lift is like from the set up through the lifting motion to the finish, you're visualizing the process. Everyone visualizes differently.

Figure out which way you visualize and what details are naturally included and emphasized in your visualizations. Then to sharpen your visualization skills, try to visualize in a different way. You may find that you visualize better with a different method. A simple way to alter your visualization method is as follows. For the sake of this example, let us say that you daydream from an associated point of view, meaning through your own eyes. First, have a short daydream about yourself. See it through your own eyes as you normally do. Then recreate your daydream from another point of view, outside of you, from the point of view of a television camera. Follow your daydream through and watch the scene with you in it. Try this method with a lift. Daydream your lift from within your own eyes. Then reverse your point of view from associated to dissociated (first person to third person). This will look like recording your lift with a digital camera. Attempt the lift in your mind and then go to the platform. Don't immediately rule out that one perspective isn't effective for you. It's possible that a bit more practice with a new perspective could lead to better results than your original perspective. Once you can manage shifting your perspective in visualizing, alter the process/results visualization. Go back to your daydream or your low weight lift. Perform the visualization. If you fully visualized the scene from beginning to end, including the lift, imagine only the ending. See yourself victorious. If you usually see the end of the lift only, contemplate all those other details. See the set up and the lift, feel the weight and the stress, and hear your buddies cheering. This part might be tedious. Sometimes it's hard to change a thought process, but give it a try. Have the daydream, but see the entire lift. You might also find that you visualize the set up and the finish but not the lift. You might visualize only certain parts. In other words, your natural or your best method of visualizing might be mixed methods. That's fine. Some people visualize like a movie, part of the process, from different people's point of view with different soundtracks. These visualization models are rules-of-thumb to guide you in improving your mind.

For a totally different frame of reference

Once you're capable of changing perspectives and paths, add them together. If you usually daydream the entire process in the third person, imagine only the result from the first person. If you like sharpening your mind, attempt to be proficient at all four combinations in your day dreams and visualizations:

- first person—process
- first person—result
- third person—process
- third person—result

Some words of caution

One day at the gym, pick a lift, set up the bar, load some weight, and then give each method a try. Visualizing takes as much practice as lifting to become proficient, so get your reps in. Learn to visualize and test your methods under safe, controlled, low intensity conditions. Visualization can be distracting and therefore dangerous. It can actually lower your focus if you aren't used to it or do it wrong. 'Thinking' and doing the wrong kind of thinking before a lift can crush you. Don't try something totally new at a crucial moment. This is for two reasons. One, we don't rise to occasions. We default to our level of training, meaning we do what we know how to do. Second, introducing new, unknown variables can be disastrous. You wouldn't make an exotic, spicy dish that you've never tried before on the eve of your next big meet. These are things that wait to haunt us until we get under the load. Therefore, a low to medium load is better when learning to visualize.

Level of detail

Let us walk one step further with the methods of visualization. Imagine yourself about to do a lift. Where are you? What does the **platform** look like? What lift are you about to perform? What music are you listening to? How do you feel physically and mentally? When visualizations are drawn from experience, you'll have more concrete details to include. There are numerous details involved in constructing a reality in your head, but you need to figure out what the relevant details are. During certain visualizations, enormous detail can help, such as when you aren't in a lifting session and you're working on your visualization skills. If you're about to do a lift, you will need to see the lift without distractions or things that take away your focus. Examine what the most powerful things are in your thoughts. What senses, emotions, and thoughts dominate when you think about and then successfully execute a lift? Are there any details you could add or modify that are positive cues? Put these to work in your future visualizations as emotional cues that will inspire your mind and ignite your nerves and muscles to complete the task.

Further application

The methods of visualization described are applicable to sets as well as to singles. Through greater experience, I began to see a set as a string of singles. For me, it's easier to get through a set with good form if I see each rep individually. When performing a single, there is only one 'first rep,' which happens to be all the work of the entire set. In a set of multiple reps, there is still only one 'first rep,' but then there are also the rest of the reps that each require as much attention and effort. Visualization can help separate the larger goal of completing the set into several small goals of completing each rep. This is how visualization skills carry over into goal setting. These visualization combinations can be used to help you identify each step in achieving a higher goal. For example, to set a class record at your next meet, you have to do things other than just see yourself on the podium with a medal. You have to train, you need a program, you need to perform each lift, you need sleep and recovery, and you need to work on joint mobility. You can and should visualize it all.

Why bother?

Visualization works. However you do it, whatever method you use, and whatever perspective your imagination works from, you can accomplish more by using positive thinking. Visualization is a simple, convenient, easy, legal performance and lift assist. Your hopes and dreams make a difference because they're the starting place of action. Visualization in lifting is a simple act of picturing what you're about to do and then making it happen. It isn't witchcraft or folklore. Strengthen your mind and shape your victory.

Part 2: Ritual Reinforcement

Introduction

In the grand scheme of fitness and adaptation, there may be such a thing as wasted reps. In terms of technical mastery, every rep counts. Each rep and set is a lesson in how to and how not to do something. There is an adage "practice makes perfect." This is a half truth. The full story is "perfect practice makes perfect." You will get out what you put in. You don't rise to the occasion; you default to your level of training. In order to practice perfectly and reach new heights of skill and strength, you need to know what you are practicing and be fully engaged mentally as well as physically. Following, I will explain the importance of engaging in the ritual that accompanies visualization.

The approach

You never get to do this rep again. There are infinite tomorrows until you make a choice and then that means there is only one now that creates one yesterday. This is your only chance. How do you want this set to go down? Are you going to 'get it over with' or are you going to 'crush this set?' Will you worry about selling tickets to the gun show or will you face each rep with the focus of a third attempt? There is a Japanese martial art known as Kyudo, 'the way of the bow,' or in the reductionist view of the west, simply archery. What you should strive to have in common with the Kyudoka or Japanese archer is the focus on the target. To the archer, the universe disappears around the bull's eye. That bull's eye becomes the only object in existence and the archer becomes one with it. Your rep must be that bull's eye. I suppose Chevy Chase's character from *Caddyshack* would say "Be the bar." How do you establish such an intense mindset that is virtually a trance state? You need a ritual. A ritual is a predetermined and choreographed set of thoughts and actions that have deep meaning to you. You probably already have a ritual for lifting. If you go silent, put on your headphones and put on your wraps. Then you have a ritual.

Why is a ritual important?

The ritual is symbolic. The actions you perform mean something to your subconscious mind. We have a part of our mind that influences our thoughts and performance but that we have limited conscious access to.

One of the ways in which we can tap into the performance enhancement potential that our mind offers is to establish a ritual composed of things we only do in the gym before the lift. For example, wrapping, belting, and chalking. Wrapping your wrists, putting on your belt, and chalking your hands and back are powerful stimuli for two reasons—you only do them in the gym before a lift, and the feelings of wrapping, belting, and **chalking** are heavily associated with the experience of the lift. The wraps, belt, and chalk are 'anchors,' things that bring you into a specific mental, emotional, and physical state when experienced. The mental association between your 'gym anchors' and anything other than lifting are nonexistent. These anchors likely remind you of nothing else…unless you do the dishes and mow the lawn wearing your gear (no judgment here). When you put the equipment on, you go into a specific state because the equipment is a serious reminder of what is to come.

Make your ritual more powerful

If you want to make your ritual work more to enhance your performance under the bar, here are some things you can do:

1. Organize a simple ritual that you like
2. Be aware of the timing
3. Set up the environment to support your ritual

First, have a ritual and try to follow the order. For example, when it's time for the next squat set, I walk away from any conversation or whatever it is I'm doing. I will pace and focus on breathing. Then I put my belt on, with the prong in the first hole. Then I wrap my wrists. Then I chalk my hands. Then I tighten the belt. Then I stand in front of the bar and visualize the set. Then I put my hands on the bar and focus my gaze on the bar while becoming more mentally focused. Then I get under the bar, get set, and walk it out slowly. Physically setting up correctly under the bar is of paramount importance. Matt Gary (2012 USAPL coach of the year) and Suzy Gary (USAPL Powerlifting Hall of Fame) both place tremendous importance on setting up perfectly and without rushing. Above all parts of the ritual, setting up and walking out are the most powerful parts. A tight set up and an easy stand up indicate that I'm about to do some good lifts.

The walk out will push that into reality. Then I set my breath, and right before I squat, I remind myself that this is a single rep. In between reps, I reload. I remind myself again that each rep is a single. Matt Gary, coach and co-owner of SSPT, gave me the idea to visualize loading a rifle, as each rep is a single shot. Now, at the top of each rep, I think of that, which has the added benefit of creating a short pause to reset for the next rep. I do every rep of every lift in a similar fashion. I have specific things I do in a specific order that all flow together and put me in a strong state of mind. Second, be aware of the timing of your rests. If you need to keep on a schedule, pay attention to the clock or set an alarm. The last thing you want to do is rush through your ritual. The ritual needs your devotion and careful attention for it to work. Also, don't take too long. Every ritual is powerful within certain parameters such as the time, location, and anchors. Think of this as 'stimulus and response' of your mind. Third, set up your environment to support your ritual. Have your equipment easily accessible. Have the right music ready to go. I like to squat heavy right at the beginning of Iron Maiden's 'Alexander the Great,' when the intro bursts into the galloping drums right before the singing starts (another ritual). Have the bar loaded, unless loading is a part of the rite. Know where the clock is. Stay hydrated. Have an obstacle-free walk to the rack. Stay away from the gym sewing bees and social clubs. Move equipment if you're allowed and if you prefer a different configuration. You know your favorite parts of the gym and favorite equipment. In other words, physically set up your environment so that your ritual and lift can flow together.

The visualization part

The hidden theme is how to make the most out of visualization by putting your mind in a state where visualization will have more effect. The ritual is used to put you in a tuned-in mental state. That mental state is conducive to creative visualization and positive thinking. You may experiment where in the ritual you put the visualization. I tend to visualize my next lift during the rest before and also during the set up.

Chaos or calm?

Everyone reacts differently under the stress of resistance training. Some people can't wait to get the lift while other people become anxious and experience negative feelings that can become overwhelming. What matters is what you do with the experience. Like making each rep count, your road to mastery is paved by how you integrate that emotional response into the experience. People who have a hard time processing, accepting, and resolving stress can become stuck in a negative mental state and experience trauma. You can overcome emotional and mental barriers by using rituals and visualization. Just like visualization though, you might have to experiment with your ritual to find out what works best for you.

The warning

Try to avoid becoming superstitious or adopting superstitious practices. The purpose of the ritual is to get you correct in the head before you perform a dangerous act that will also serve to increase your performance by giving you total control and responsibility. The one differentiating factor between strength sports and other sports is that gravity works the same way, every day, in every rep. In other sports, the other guy might have a better day or land a lucky shot on you. In lifting, the only variable is you. The locus of control is in you. There are no lucky wraps, lucky bars, lucky shirts, lucky squat racks, or lucky anything. While these items serve as anchors, mental reminders that put you into a productive mental state, they aren't the sole determiners of your performance. What if you have to use the gym's common use wraps, your favorite bar is in use, or your shirt is in the wash? Does a lack of lucky rabbits' feet make you a weakling? No! The locus of control is in you. You are strong because you **train**. Superstition removes your mental strength, which can limit your physical strength. Adopt ritual practices that enable you to reach your potential, not hold you to a limited amount of success and failure.

Conclusion

The roles of the central nervous system and neural activation in sport performance have been addressed at length. The practice of ritual and visualization is one more aspect of the nervous system that can't be ignored. Apply these ideas to your training and put yourself in a high performance state. Your mind helps you gain power over matter so use the ritual to create stronger and clearer visualizations of your lifts and greater focus under stress.

"Relax your mind, tighten your body, breathe deep, focus to clarity, lift, and win."

-

Things You'll Need

- Tape recorder
- Comfortable chair

Instructions

1. **Increasing Strength Through Self Hypnosis**

    - 1

        Relax. The key to self hypnosis is the ability to relax your mind and body enough that it is able to fall into a hypnotic trance or state. The easiest way to do this is through controlled breathing, relaxing visualizations, or repeating a relaxing mantra.

Ideally, you should relax your mind and body for about 15-20 minutes prior to attempting self hypnosis.

- 2

    Begin self hypnosis. One way to achieve self hypnosis is through concentrating on affirmations and visualizing what you want. This is a light version of self hypnosis in that you are in a light hypnotic state and in control. For immediate strength training, you can visualize your muscles getting larger, exercising the individual muscle areas and repeating to yourself that you are getting stronger and stronger. You should notice your confidence will have increased and experience a feeling of empowerment. You also may feel stronger.

- 3

    Try deep trance hypnosis. The way to have the best immediate results is to attempt to fall into a deep hypnotic state. This is the state used in hypnotic stage shows and hypnotherapy. In this state, you are not in control or aware of your surroundings and instead are focused on the voice of the person giving directions. In this case, the directions will be provided by a tape recorded script that you prepared beforehand.

- 4

    Tape a hypnosis script. There are many hypnotic induction scripts available on the Internet. This script will bring you into the hypnotic state. A second script will focus on increasing your muscle strength. These scripts are more difficult to find, but they are out there or you can create your own. You should focus on you becoming stronger, blocking the pain mechanism, increasing adrenaline production, and visualizing larger muscles. A final script will include the opposite technique of induction and will bring you out of the hypnotic state. You should create the tape or CD in such a way that all the scripts lead naturally into each other.

- 5

    Reinforce every few days. A hypnotic command or suggestion needs to be reinforced on a regular basis in order to keep working.

    If you notice a substantial strength increase, you can change the script to make your muscles even larger. You should repeat the script every few days to make sure the commands and suggestions continue to be effective and after several weeks the need for reinforcement should diminish.

Read more: How to Improve Overall Strength Overnight Through Self Hypnosis | eHow.com http://www.ehow.com/how_5646627_improve-overnight-through-self-hypnosis.html#ixzz2BmBNB800

Inspiration Gallery

Alan Mead, circa 1924. Alan lost his leg in WW I and decided to take action by lifting heavy as his method of recovery where most people would have made excuses and given up! There are NO excuses for modern day Gladiators! An "endurance" performance in the straight arm pullover was made about 1925 by the English physical culturist and muscular phenomenon Alan P. Mead (182 lbs.). He raised a 70 lb. barbell 70 times in succession. Regrettably, I have no information on what Mead could do either in chinning or dipping, although he doubtless practiced both these exercises in his well-equipped public gymnasium in London. Like Joe Nordquest, Mead had lost one of his lower legs below the knee, and this loss of 10 or 12 lbs. made it easier for him in some exercises where he lifted his own weight. Too, in instances like those of Mead and Nordquest, the performer's lifts should be related not to the actual bodyweight, but to what that weight would probably be if the missing portion of the limb or limbs were restored.

Luke Iams, of the "Wild Bunch of West Virginia"

My "Forgotten Secrets of the Culver City Westside Barbell club Revealed" book has a chapter dedicated to Luke & the rest of that crew.

"Peanuts" West performing his favorite exercise, the squat. He has the type of leverage which permits him to work most efficiently flatfooted, with no heel blocks, and recently made a national record for the 198 lb. class at a San Diego contest, of 585½. He also made a bench press of 385 and a dead lift of 585 which gave him a 1555½ total. Photo by Goldman.

"Peanuts" West and His Muscle Power Factory

And speaking of the Culver City crew, it's most renowned member, Bill West had to be one of the most inspirational guys ever!

How about this guy with his incredible pulling power, as described in my "King Squat, Rise to Power" book:

Bob Peoples

Allentown area legend Fred Glass, defying both age & gravity yet again.

This gentleman was probably responsible for launching more strength athlete's careers than just about anyone....

John C. Grimek

Unknown iron warrior

The Squat Heard Around the World... Joe Bradley's 650 at 132 at the 1980 Worlds! Here are Herb Glossbrenner's comments about this month's all time list: "Mighty Joe Bradley leads the pack with his 'Bridgesgarian' squat, which will probably still be intact as we cross the threshold of the next century. Heath leads this year with 5th best of all time - 565 He is now just one notch behind the magical, mystical 575 of our own Judd Biasiotto Of the TOP 10 Best, I personally witnessed Ken Westbrook's 556. It was impeccable and a lift to truly be proud of. Lady Mary Warman made the Top 50, a remarkable achievement, and became the lightest woman to squat 500. Oldest mark among the 100 best is Joe Grosson's 479 made 15 years ago Nearly 50 athletes made 500. Veteran Ernesto Milian is still in the TOP 25."

One of the strongest "little guys" ever!

What lifter has not been inspired by this guy??

> THE DISTANCE BETWEEN YOUR DREAMS AND REALITY IS CALLED DISCIPLINE.

Thank you for purchasing the book. I hope you enjoyed reading it. For more of my books, please check out my website,

http://www.christianiron.com/Pages/VaultofSecrets.aspx

They are also available on Amazon

Also check out my Face book page

https://www.facebook.com/pages/Forgotten-Strength-Secrets

My powerlifting Team's page:

https://www.facebook.com/TwinCityBarbellClub

5939510R00139

Printed in Great Britain
by Amazon.co.uk, Ltd.,
Marston Gate.